TENDER

D. Clifford Hill

Charnel Ground Publishing
San Francisco

Copyright © 2014 by D. Clifford Hill

Disclaimer: Although this is a work of nonfiction, the names of those mentioned have been altered.

All rights reserved. No part of this publication may be reproduced, distributed or transmitted in any form or by any means, including photocopying, recording, or other electronic or mechanical methods, without the prior written permission of the publisher, except in the case of brief quotations embodied in critical reviews and certain other non-commercial uses permitted by copyright law. For permission requests, email the publisher at: charnelgroundpub@gmail.com

www.CharnelGroundPub.com

Edited by Mailyn Von Qualen: mvq@corselan.com
Consultant: Paula Hendricks
Book and Cover Design by Greg Christian
Original Portrait by Akira Beard

Tender by D. Clifford Hill -- First Edition
ISBN 978-0-9915151-0-3

TENDER

Dedicated to George Birimisa
"Be Honest"

TENDER

PART ONE

ONE

I know lonely when I see it. There is hollowness about a man, an echo in every gesture, a salty taste in whatever he devours with those sad eyes of his. He sits across from me in a near empty Tuesday night train heading downtown. His loneliness is telling in the way he leans his head into the stretch of his raised arm clinging tightly through brown clenched fingers to a white streaked silver pole running from the side of his seat to the ceiling above him. It tells in the crooked cradling arm around his lap-ladled backpack and the wide splay of his fingers curving its sagging bottom that he hungers for some company. That could be my ass beneath his hand. That could be my hip beneath his cradle. That could be my arm feeling the moist masculine warmth of his tired exhale at the end of a long day.

He appears lonely in the shift from one buttock to another on the hard plastic seat, cheek leaning into cheek, legs crossing and uncrossing again seeking the rest and comfort found only in the spooning company of another on an old couch or better yet on the soft of a queen size bed. I close my eyes for a moment, feel his pelvis pushing into my backside, his knees curling into the cups of my knees, his skinny arm jointed along my waistline while the warmth of his palm spreads across my belly. He is lonely. I can feel it in my quickened pulse when the stare of our eyes touch from opposite sides of the train and then dash away, mine falling into my hands folding into each other like a lady applying lotion at Macy's makeup counter.

His eyes go somewhere; I wish I knew so I could follow. I wonder if he is looking at me again. I raise my stare cautiously. He has a crazy look about him. His eyes aren't in agreement with his mouth. They push from their sockets in search of something, anything, scrambling along the gray floor amidst orange peels and shelled sunflower seeds. A Starbuck's coffee cup rolls in circles, his eyes are there to follow. He lifts his gaze to the fluorescent glow running the length of the train, the whites absorbing light and becoming whiter, red rimmed lids flickering under the tension. He stares into the light for nearly a full minute and all the while his rich full lips pull back into a smile, pull back into a bone thin face, the face of a meth addict who hasn't eaten or slept since last Friday night, an addict constantly in the street or online in search of big dicks and deep asses. Or it could be the face of an HIV-positive man who has been on 'the cocktail' for years beyond his life expectancy. Hollowed cheeks, facial wasting they call it. Ugly, I think as I turn to the reflection of my own gaunt and wasting expression in the window at my side. Fucking ugly! Looking sixty when I am only forty-nine! He won't take any interest in me. Twenty years of living dis-eased. But look at him; he is some kind of sexy with those high cheek bones and sharp jaw lines. He smiles into the white of the light. I sink defeated into my seat and lean the side of my head into the cold of the window.

    Stations pass but I hardly notice; in the dark when lights get shorted on the train they flash on and off, on and off. I catch him smiling at me, not a full smile, just a turn at the corners of his mouth. He's smiling at me and his eyes have lost their wide-eyed searching desperation and he watches me now, sexy side-eyed and relaxed. His arm lifts and stretches across the back of the seat, his legs spread wide, head tilted, his tongue slipping through lips I want to whisper my name. He may be crazy, he may be lonely, he is probably an addict, a thief, or a hustler. But then, so am I in the short stretch of imagination. Having once had a career, a paycheck and a 401K doesn't mean shit; everything blows apart just as my life did with two gunshot blasts. Stability flutters like pigeons hopping around scattered bread crumbs on the sidewalk; desperation drives me to borrowing hope from dreams of my past while stealing desire and pleasure to escape the pain of now, the trembling uncertain future ahead. A quickened wind blows cold and lonely through my heart as I watch him watching me. Desire keeps my eyes fixed on his every move as the wind sinks into my belly.

"He can't be crazier than any of the men I meet in this fucked up town" I justify to myself. I lift from my seat as the familiar white marble floors of the Civic Center station slow to a stop outside the door. He stands as his eyes fall, taking me in from the wear of my boots to the wool cap on my head. Quietly I say to myself, "Come on baby, let me take you home and take care of you for awhile." I wonder if he sees me talking to myself like this. If he follows me I'll invite him up for soup and toast, lemon pound cake for dessert, I'll draw a bath if he needs one. I feel his eyes watching my fingers bending one after another against my jaw. Pop goes the knuckle, pop goes another. Pop, pop, pop.

"Hey man, you sell me a smoke for a quarter?" His words from behind me lift more quickly than the steps of the long escalator we ride.

I turn sharp, too quickly, not cool I think to myself as I face him. I didn't realize he was so close, two steps down. "I, I don't smoke."

"Cool." He nods, keeping his eyes on me. "There's a store up the street I can buy one at."

"Yea I know the store. Four-fifty a pack or twenty-five cents per cigarette. Someone's makin' some fast change. When I smoked I used to buy mine there." I over explain. I don't pull my gaze from him.

"Sometimes all ya need is one smoke to cut the edge." He looks away, digging in his pockets.

"You got an edge?"

"Maybe." Chin to chest he smiles up at me through skinny brows. "Hey, ya got a quarter?" I look at him with the unspoken question he quickly answers with the shrug of his shoulders. "I thought I had a quarter but I don't." He has stopped digging in his jeans. Perhaps I'll wash those while he is taking a bath. I push deep into my own pocket and rub against the hardening of my dick; two steps below me he notices the rounding curve in the crotch of my jeans. He smiles like he does.

"Here." I hand him two dimes and a nickel.

We walk in silence, my thoughts three steps behind us. His shoulders push his stride along much like Maynard's used to. The proud of his chin tells him which direction to turn, the shine of his brow smiles when he isn't smiling at all but lost in a thought in the crack of the sidewalk; just like Maynard. "Didn't your mama teach you not to stare?" He dashes a smile to cut the edge of his words.

"She probably never seen anything so damn sexy."

"Really?" He stops his step. I say fuck you with a chuckling mind and keep on walking.

"Don't let it go to your head." I say over my shoulder.

"Too damn late."

Maynard's laughter comes haunting as the play in me falls away; lost I am in the headlights streaming toward me and this man as we walk up Hyde. Maynard's entire body laughed, his feet would dance while his hands shook the air. He would bend over and slap his palms on his knees, his mouth open wide exposing the pink of his gums, the length of his tongue. His roar could stop traffic if it wasn't for his hand smothering it down. I am lost in recollections walking outside the caverns of the Orpheum Theater, the library, the vacant federal building; all the world is an echo as is Maynard's laughter; Maynard once so full of joy, Maynard my office confidant, Maynard dead in my stead; a midnight fucking mantra walking home along Hyde.

My man from the train dances up to my side. Memories want to burn into tears but I won't let them, at least not with sexy at my side; my throat closes, my chest tightens, I don't allow myself to breathe. I cannot look his way. No tears not now. It is my fault, it should have been me. No tears not now. My teeth clench hard. I shouldn't have run, I should have stayed in the office even though every bone in my body cried of danger, screamed in alarm. Get out! No tears not now. My attention falls into the gutter, tires of parked cars, empty Dasani water bottles, plastic bags and food containers. Cigarette butts. His nine-year-old boy missing his daddy every goddamn day . . . not now! Just shut the fuck up! I jerk in a turn; I take him in again, my heart pounding fierce. I push tension down in swallows. What's his name? I want to ask but words won't come and shame halts my attempt in that I have forgotten it already. Did I even fucking ask?

"Where do you stay?" His lips move, his words I hear, his smile waits for my response.

A sweep of the streets with my eyes reminds me where I am. "Up, uh, up on O'Farrell."

I look over my shoulder along the stretch of block we have come and wonder how long I have been gone like I go; the timeless tunnels of my mind drag me down and deep, thoughts otherwise come from a question I am asked, a direction I am given, a compliment I am unable to return. I shake myself back to his question, my response, my question. "And you?"

"Oh, down South of Market." The wave of his hand in the air is an unmeasurable distance. I assume the Shelter at Fifth and Bryant since specifics are dashed and a silence hangs in the air. My assumptions have been wrong before. His black coat is frayed at the cuffs, worn gray at the elbows, jeans too big, t-shirt graying, he does not shy from the street or the Tenderloin, he knew the cigarette store, buys his smokes one at a time.

"What do you do?" My skepticism asks.

"For a living?" His eyebrows dart to the serious of the question. He does not wait for my response. "I am a student."

"Really?" My enthusiasm hits too high. I can't help myself, was expecting something different, something like General Assistance, SSI or the hustle of men I run into in the street; a five dollar blow job or the buy-me-alcohol-all-night-guy who's flirt is harder than his limp whiskey dick.

"What do you study?"

"Right now Arabic and poetry and dance at UC Berkeley." I stop in my stride. "I want to study economics theory though." Realizing my lag his eyes trail the ground between his side and my feet. "Come on, I want a cigarette." His smile shines the same as those big eyes of his; a quick flash of white in the darkness of the street. He smiles the smile of Maynard. I shake my thought. I look to the ground to not go tunneling again. Urine is a wet line I step over on the sidewalk. I notice the flattened backs of his shoes, old dress shoes, thrift store worn. His knapsack sags low his back. I wonder if he is lying.

    The light is red at the corner. He turns into me, his lips nearly mouth my ear, his chest hints pressing against mine. I want to bite the curve of his neck. So what if he is lying. His seduction whispers "What-do-you-do?" The wind of him sends me racing. I smell him through the pores of my skin, chill bumps rising, shivers shaking me down. My eyes fix on the corner across from us, Chinese Food and Donuts, never noticed it in the Tenderloin before, in the Mission yes, still it doesn't make sense.

    "I, uh, am not working . . . right now." I smile at my dodge of his play. How long has it been I ask myself in case he asks? A year? A year and a half? Chow mein and maple glazed. I think it has been a year but I struggle with time. I look down the street even though he is still in my ear. Old fashioned was my favorite when I was a kid.

    "I got something for you to work."

    I smile and drop into the warm air of his words. The light changes to green and he is well into the street headed with his wide eyes and smile straight for Chinese Food and Donuts.

    I hate sprinkles. I never liked cake donuts either. A year and a half and I can't even remember what month it is, what season it is or if the sun shined at all today. My mother loved cinnamon rolls. She warmed hers in the oven. I look up into the sky expecting to see stars like I did when I was a kid, half expecting them to tell me the season. My mother used to say if

I saw the sky at night full of stars it was a guarantee the next day was going to be nice. But you never see stars in the Tenderloin. It was sunny the day Maynard was killed. That was in May.

    I stand in the light of a street lamp waiting for him to buy his cigarette. I think to myself, I am that elderly Chinese lady across the street who bends as far as she can with a long metal stick into the city garbage can on the corner, poking and stirring amidst the garbage in hopes of finding a recyclable can or bottle. She shakes out the remaining fluid of a can into the gutter, smashes the can beneath the sole of her shoe while wiping her face on the long sleeve of her shirt. Collecting the smashed can into a plastic bag tied to a long wooden broom handle, she moves onto the next corner. I drop my eyes into the trash strewn gutter. My arrogance disgusts me. I am no different than anyone else on this street; I am just a drunken, depressed jaded old queen who sits in my rent controlled apartment high on the edge of the Tenderloin giving head to a beer bottle. I stumble out at midnight with a fierce hard-on with the lure of lemon pound cake for a late night snack, the comfort of a warm bed and a promise of breakfast in the morning.

    The shadows of Hyde host the hustle of dealers, Bic lighters flash at the ends of crack pipes, laughter rises from a doorway we pass, huddles of the lost curl into themselves on laid out cardboard, milk crates are stools, dice are thrown, transistor radios scratch, neon beer signs are bright and colorful over their heads through the night.

    We walk in silence, not an anxious silence but a

comfortable one; my mind is quiet, our steps are in sync even though our direction has not been discussed. I like this guy. I move through the clouded exhale of his cigarette smoke. The thought of tobacco on his breath sends chills racing through me.

"Is the smoke cutting that edge of yours?"

"For now." He smiles that half-smile and side-eyes me.

"You hungry? Would you like some cake?"

TWO

In my mind of yesterday I stand at a bus stop even though I don't need to take the bus. Young black men gather listening to hip hop and rap from a boom box sitting on top a beaten old newspaper box on the edge of the extra wide sidewalk. Three older black men lean the wall of an apartment building across from them; two others sit on the ground. I stand as near as I allow, want to breathe in their masculinities, feel the calm strength of their no need to hurry, beg with my presence the chance to converse, if nothing else catch an eye of interest. I pace a few circles to act as if impatient, flip my phone, check the time, check for calls I know I haven't received. My eyes try to avoid what I want to watch; don't want to come off as some old sleazy fucker. So I steal glimpses of the men, savor pauses and then jump away across the street to the comings and goings of disinterest; tight legged hipster boys on bikes, lost tourists clenching their open maps. The bus comes, passengers unload, no one gets on. We aren't waiting on the bus.

    I follow the passion of their want in their eyes, a slow ride cruising by with shiny chrome, dark windows and wide rims, a woman curving their imaginations to discomfort, skateboarders gravelling down the street. I don't really listen to what they talk about; I simply ride the rhythm of their words as if they are being spoken to me while my eyes are closed.

    The flash of an oversized white t-shirt jumps into the rap of music in a sidewalk square, shoulders and chin hammer the beat into the air punctuating the tight of sharp rhyming words. The others step back and allow him his minute. Watching, I keep a distance, at times looking beyond them for the bus I am not waiting on. The singing white t-shirt stops and stumbles out of the circle of attention allowed him, he steps toward me, I feel the heat sweating from him even though he is a few feet away. His baggy pants are belted around his thighs. My heart pounds fierce and closes my throat too tight to swallow. There is a rush in knowing he might go off on me. "WHAT THE FUCK ARE YOU LOOKIN' AT OLD MAN?!" He knows I am watching I convince myself, that is why he comes dancing so damn close, challenging me. I wish I could claim just one glance, one meeting of the eyes, one brush of his wind to take with me and run. I turn my shoulder away but feel him checking me out. Don't I just wish he took the slightest fucking interest in me?

Black men know, straight or gay, when a white boy wants it or so I've been told by the brothers in my bed. Never knew I was so damn transparent. I listen to this Tenderloin rap star's voice as his words run on end to each other. What would he say and how would he say it after the last scream of orgasm was muffled by the gasping of air, his nakedness lying weak and defeated on top of me. "Dang baby!" is all I long to hear. Just say it. "Dang baby!" Then I'll feed him dinner. I can't help it, it's just my shit.

The sweet of lemon pound cake is sweet for a few heartbeats, the draw off a twenty-five cent cigarette softens the edge only to a point. Darnell, the man from the train in my bed gets too fucking serious with me after hours of fucking. "I know I'm not as endowed as other men" he states looking direct into my eyes. His jaw grinds. He pushes his dick deeper into me even though he just came. "I know my six and a half inches don't stand to the nine you want." He challenges me with a stink eye.

"It ain't the size that matters. It's what you do with what you got." I reach to his neck and pull him in, our mouths opening and hungering, eating each other then pulling away. His flat stomach breathes into mine.

"I don't have no trouble not being endowed like the others." Repeating his point his jaw continues to grind. He pushes deeper inside me still. "No baby, I ain't finished yet." He reads my mind. My eyes fall to the stretch of his collarbone reaching into the curved round of his shoulder, the depth between his biceps and his chest. His smell is the bitter most decent men repel from, the smell I bury my face into. "Man, size is the last you need to be worrying about. What you just did with six and a half inches most nine inches can't touch."

"I said I'm alright with not being endowed." He drives his point again with sharp eyes staring into me. I let his words slide. His skinny tongue circles the wide of his mouth and I feel his belly pull up from mine as he swallows deep. He falls into a mindless stare into the midnight blue of the room; it is the same endless stare as on the train.

"Hey man" I say. "You alright?" He continues to lie on top of me, his cum wetted dick still hard inside of me, mine still hard between our pressed bodies, waiting for its turn to scream. He stares. I watch and know he is gone like I go, but then again he seems to go a bit further. I don't say anything more, just lay still and wait for his return.

In the darkening room an hour later I rest my head on his chest. His arm wraps around my shoulder. I feel safe, protected. I remember back to 1968 or 69 when I was eight or nine years old, my father got lost driving the family through the streets of West Oakland, our white Ford Fairlane station wagon dashing in circles. "Damn these streets" my father swore under his breath until the fourth or fifth wrong turn and he pounded the same words with the butt of his hand into the blue steering wheel. "Damn these streets!" Just ahead a group of black men stood on the corner. "Roll up your windows and lock your doors!" My father's panicked words slapped me from my lost gazing wonder. I had never seen him afraid of anything, nothing at all. "Now!" His eyes darted crazy from his boys in the rear view mirror to the street ahead. "I said now damn it!" I grabbed hold of the window crank, looked out my window but could not see the reason for panic. I slowly gave it a quarter turn.

Black men stood along the sidewalk outside of a church, smiling, talking, laughing with one another. They were dressed in suits. There were no black men in the town I lived in, at least not in my experience. I had only seen them on TV. Howard Cossell had interviewed one that morning during an Oakland Raiders game. Out my window I lost myself in curiosity. What about them was I supposed to be afraid of? I saw no need to roll up my window and lock my door. "Lock your goddamn door!" my father shouted over his shoulder again as he white knuckled the steering wheel in search of the quickest freeway entrance. "And roll up that damn window!" My mother tried to turn around in the front seat but my father extended his arm to stop her. The men on the corner did not look at us as we drove by, in spite of our faces pressed up against the rising window as I cranked as slow as I could. The black men just kept laughing and smiling amongst themselves. One man patted the other's back while shaking his hand.

"Boys. Don't stare" my mother insisted.

"Goddamn city is going to get us killed!" My father continued his rant.

Darnell sighs into deeper sleep, wraps his other arm around me and pulls me closer still. I reach into the warm wet hairy mass of his crotch and fill my hand with the dick he drove me to ecstasy with. We sleep through the night clinging to one another like children.

THREE

Knotted wires beneath my desk are too afraid to be undone, too afraid of the potential disconnect, too afraid of endless confusion, endless guilt, I should have been more attentive to their laying. My gut is exactly what I surmise, wires and knots and dust motes and should haves and fear. I should get in there and pull out the stereo wires from the phone wires from the lamp wires from the computer wires from the printer, the scanner, the power strip, but overwhelm snarls my assertion. Every corner of my studio houses the procrastination of guilt; cardboard boxes of rusty scrap metal found in the streets holding intention to become objects of art, drawers in the kitchen full of useless gadgets people have given me through the years; an avocado slicer, Buddha Jell-O molds, a hash brown potato dicer, shit I will never use but hold onto out of some sort of sick obligation like they are coming tomorrow to make sure I still have them. Next to my desk a musty leather suitcase of old family photographs, pictures of cousins and second cousins whose names I will never recall, school pictures of my nieces and nephews, studio shots, blue backdrops, they never fucking smile, I never fucking care. Every year I ask myself why? Either side of me rise stacks of unfinished manuscripts, the unrealized dream of getting published repeated now too many times to care anymore. Masturbation if you ask me. My gaze falls below again, hesitant to jump into the heap, my eyes follow one wire curling up and then down and around and under, losing myself in thoughts of many months passed, perhaps two years now, losing count.

    He stares into a deep hole in the floor between our three pair of feet, six shoes in a circle pointing uncomfortably to the center, his toes tapping then not, then tapping again, mine curling in my boots until they are numb. "Agenda items?" she asks. The hole in the floor is only apparent to his strained bloodshot eyes, bulging eyes, fish eyes, eyes you can't escape. I wonder if he is looking for agenda there in the hole of his mind but know better of his rage having caught glimpses of it before. I know he is quietly building fires and defenses, stoking coals, strengthening walls, preparing arguments, readying himself for a good fight. I watched him smoke once while he explained in detail why Jockey underwear was responsible for male infertility. "Testicles were designed by God to hang low and away from the body." His dead-on look challenged me with no need of words. A grin cautioned my unshaven face at his sudden religion. He took another deep drag, allowing the pause between his thoughts to linger in the air as smoke shot from his black-flared nostrils in a steady stream. He looked away with squinted eyes as if reading a research article. "Ninety-eight point six degrees is too hot for sperm to thrive." His lips punched his words and his fingertips pinched the filter nearly flat. My eyebrows lifted in my nod of understanding, my futile attempt at interest. "In my neighborhood growing up, that was all that was sold; white Jockey underwear by rich old white men." His eyes glared the street with his assertion, his words landed there just beyond the curb. His accusation turned to me before his eyes captured mine, my face now drawn in pale disbelief. "They didn't want us making no babies." He dragged one last time on that flat darkened cigarette butt and dropped it to smother under the sole of his shoe and ground it hard into the sidewalk. He kept grinding it as if waiting for a response from me. There wasn't one. I was too focused on calming the creep of discomfort in me, my own shoes desiring to grind fear into the sidewalk.

Watching him stare into that hole I am reminded he never takes directions from me; his resistance is based on what works best for him or so he explains and since he works alone, there is no need to change. I am new to my position so I allow him his preference until I get my feet planted and steady. I half expect him to bleed into that hole, his stare intense as it is. I want to tell him to stop but the snap of him feels too close at hand. Waiting, I lean cautiously back and flash the thought of praying. Praying for what, and to what, are thoughts without ends. Clarice looks at me, I at her, we at him. We wait for him to spew but nothing comes. Our chairs have strong backs, hard seats, planted legs. I want to run. Thirty seconds is five minutes, a deep breath never finds its own exhale. Get me the fuck out of here. I want to be beyond the smothering walls of my windowless office. I want air to cool me, a wind to blow me, carry me, fly me away from here. She looks at me, I at her, we at him, Clarice and I shrug our shoulders. The violence of silence, I think to myself, a child's game, a child's defense. The hushed tremble of him shakes the room. Clarice's shoes, white Converse high tops, pigeon toward each other. Her knees pull together, balancing a clip board. Her thumb and index finger quickly butterfly a pen between them. "Well, if no one has anything, I have a few items." Six feet shuffle. One breath is not taken. Unblinking I watch him.

Clarice continues, "Grayson, despite my repeated requests, you continue to refer to our transgender clients as 'he-she's', this is not appropriate . . ."

"Lies." His interruption does not move his eyes from the hole in the floor.

"Excuse me?" Clarice's chin lifts as her ear leans to hear him correctly. Her dreads fall away from her face. Her eyes glare down her nose. My lips a hollow O of disbelief.

"Did you have something to say regarding this Grayson?" Clarice looks to me for support. Grayson is not her staff member but mine. Her agency contracts our Social Security money management services for the residents of the Ambassador Hotel, services Grayson seems to be stumbling with. I do not look to her but nod to continue as my eyes fix on his stare. Clarice catches my direction.

"On numerous occasions I have found open client files on your desk and in the common areas for other clients to see, like by the copier and fax machines. Our agency considers this is a serious breach of confidentiality and . . ."

"Lies!" Louder his voice rises. Grayson's eyes bulge wider; his tremble becomes more visible as his fingers clench the seat of his chair. His brown skin shines in sudden sweat. The core of me turns cold and hard.

". . . and on several occasions we have found the office unlocked . . ."

"LIES! LIES! LIES!"Grayson leaps to his feet.

"Grayson! Sit down!" His glare slowly turns my direction. With molars grinding I manage, "Sit down and stop calling Clarice a liar."

Grayson faces me square. Sweat beads his temples and his brow. His fist rises to punch his long, thick pointed finger into my face. "LIES! LIES! LIES!" The veins in his forehead rage. His thumb turns his punch to his chest. "I AM NOT THE PROBLEM HERE! I AM NOT THE FUCKING PROBLEM!!!!" His finger jabs one inch from my face, "You are the problem mother fucker! You are the fucking problem!" The slam of the office door shatters the cold hard place within me. I shake from my numb toes through my weak knees, my stomach turning, my shoulders hunching. My thoughts stumble and jump and dive into holes of hiding. I cannot look to Clarice who sits in her chair waiting for something from me. I have nothing to offer. My breath returns. "Sorry." I stare into the hole the center of the floor.

FOUR

Old blue metal lockers run in a long row, padlocks and vents, initials scratched into the navy surface years ago, rust in the damp, thick air. At the end of the row his audible moan drops with a thud as his bare ass hits the skinny wooden bench beneath him, the yellow plank of the bench running into the round of this big red man, thin white hair. Red from the steam room, beating off like old motherfuckers do. Sleazy old man. He buries his face in a heavily bleached terry white towel the young all American YMCA desk clerk offered him upon his arrival. He's probably had a hard-on since that exchange. His pudgy, short fingered hands scratch the coarse towel over his red skin which quickly dampens again, glistening in the light, sweating from too much heat.
    I turn and begin working the combo on my lock.

I miss and have to spin the dial again. My once a week visit to the Y tests my memory. Am I that old? 39-9-30, 30-39-9. I miss again. Fuck it! Fuck it! Fuck it! Hard I spin the dial. Save the temper for the treadmill. I fail to convince myself. Work it out. Work it out. Cut the fucker off! Calm ain't coming easy. I look down the lockers, the fat man's eyes jump from my direction to back before him. Sleazy mother fucker! How many young boys did ya beat off at in there? Scare their asses out of there? Didn't ya get enough? Fucking pathetic, now ya settling for my tired old ass? Narrowing his eyes into contrived concentration, he goes about his business as if not having trespassed at all. He pats the towel across his forehead, wipes down around his neck and back again cutting along his deep facial lines, swiping under the extra folds of skin falling from his cheeks. In a sorrowful exhale, he continues in his attempt to brush himself dry, armpits, the round of his belly, the wide of his thighs and under his knees. He can't reach his feet. Spreading his legs while lifting his gaze up and away, he plunges the white ball of towel into his crotch and rubs quickly.

 Standing naked with my locker finally open, I sort through the wad of my gym clothes catching a whiff of old musky sweat; socks, shorts, t-shirt, towel, I continue searching for that stinking white jock strap knowing that laundry is long overdue. I like stinking white jock straps, perhaps I won't wash it. I've known men to keep theirs in plastic ziplock bags so the odor doesn't dissipate. Open the bag for a good whiff. I know one queen sells his online. I wonder how much he gets? I wonder who the fuck buys them?

The old man's eyes watching me shiver my skin with annoyance. I look up, his stroking hand pauses in his crotch, his eyes jump away again. Fuck you old man! I cover my dick with my t-shirt. He tosses the towel over the door of his locker and moans as he pulls a graying pair of white Jockey underwear from the long open rectangle before him. Shaking them out, he runs the elastic waistline through his fingers until the front is in front. Lifting his foot into the air, he punches it through the leg hole then bends as best he can, stretching the other distant foot with a groan through the second leg. He shuffles the dead waistband up his wide legs and round his full ass. The elastic that grabbed his legs tight at dawn, as fresh morning underwear does, has lost its pull. The crisp grasp of cotton against his skin now sags in late afternoon. Standing, he yawns and pushes his hand down his front side, bends at the knees, sorting, shifting, adjusting, throwing me one last hopeful glance. Disgusted, I turn and dress quickly.

Five in the afternoon the Tenderloin rolls. Folks going home from work, folks dealing dollars, folks waking up to start the night ahead. Between Ellis and Eddy, young Salvadorian men stagger the sidewalk while brown sacked beers and pints of orphaned Jack Daniel's rest themselves along the curb looking like they don't belong to anyone. Early twenties, barely shaving, eight, maybe ten of them. From the depth of a black hoodie, a sharp white line of spit hits the sidewalk hard, no concern for who might walk into that shot. Tension is a thick pull in the air, a rope of sinew ready to snap. Old fags like me know to keep our eyes on anything but the wannabe men, one look mistaken and they come crashing, any excuse to fuck up an old white queen. Fucking stupid ass gang bangers. My heart races in my approach. Cool is a distance standing between men, cool is the hard of their anger they mistake for power. They shout in hip-hop ghetto. "Dat my ride right dere!" A skinny arm points into the street through the tent of an oversized black t-shirt to the flash of a car passing. His other hand grabs his sagging falling jeans in his jumping excitement. Cool gives in to a glimpse of adolescent mind. He gathers his mean, his face sterns; his eyes meet no one's.

At home after my workout the emptiness of my alone is shattered by the ringing of my phone, Sylvia reads caller I.D. To not answer will only deepen the well in me.

"Hello." For an instant I wish I hadn't answered. The how are yous and the what is new take their turns without true conviction or care.

"I met a man on a train." I wish I smoked so I could drain a deep inhale. "I can't get him out of my mind." No comment the other end of the phone line reminds she has heard this all before, too many times to care.

Sylvia's intention rubs a therapeutic burn. "What is it you're looking for?" I hate that question because I know I'll never find it even though there are times when my hope lifts from this hole in which I live and breathes the fresh cool air of dreams of possibility.

"All I want is to pack my man's lunch in the morning and hear about his day at the end of mine."

"Uh huh."

"I want to bury my face in his armpits, breathe the bitter of his sweat and feel it against the grain of mine because sweating this life out alone is just too damn hard."

"Well that's poetic." Her sarcasm is sour as the bottom of the fridge leftovers I had planned on eating. "You should think of becoming a writer."

"Thanks Sylvia." I stare at the mountain of manuscript I pour my pain into setting on the desk; poetry I have read to her, words never shared with anyone else; a whole different dream wanting to realize. Silence falls between us as my heart slips the sad slope of loneliness. Not a drop of real ripples in any of my dreams. I pause and wonder why a friendship like Sylvia's can't sustain me. We talk three times a week, we walk, arms linked to one another each time she comes to visit. We cling to one another, hold each other erect, even in our words over the phone. I shudder at the thought of us crumbling.

Sylvia is familiar with each dark edge of me because they were hers at one time; a braless hippie on the beach in Venice, California in the sixties, commune living and commune loving, a single mother to a barefoot daughter weaned on government issued baby formula and cream of wheat. She thinks the father's name began with a G, Greg, or Gary, or Guy. "Acid made that year a blur."

Smog was her protest, she dreamed of marrying the Native American man on the seventies television commercial who stood by the littered highway with polluted smoke stacked skies fuming the background. Garbage was thrown at his feet; a single tear fell down his cheek. A graying grandmother now, she still smokes pot out of the same corncob pipe she stole from her grandfather when she was sixteen. Her secrets are mine.

"All I want is companionship." My shaking words are silenced by sirens in the streets. I lift from the couch. "To be understood." I slide into the chair at my desk. "I just want to be wanted." I lift a half finished beer and wonder if it has protein. Another workout gone to waste.

"Well, do you think you'll find it online? In a bar? Or in the streets? You're like a dog that lost its sense of smell."

I fold into my knees. "I have no idea anymore." Hopeless I sound. "Look, I'm tired." I'm not. "I gotta go to bed." I turn on the computer. "Talk to you tomorrow." Time to get laid. Time for another beer. Time to sweat. My home page sweeps across the screen. How many people have a sex site as their home page?

For some reason the empty of my mind hits most hard this time of day, the sound of a coin dropping into the despair of an empty panhandler's cup, the hollow never full. I imagine most aging old queens like me probably turn on their televisions to keep them company, doze during commercials until sleep fades their lonely away. I rock in my desk chair looking out across Tenderloin roof tops like an old fucking geezer in a rocker on the front porch.

In my lonely I watch residence hotels fade their

graffiti-tagged Tenderloin colors into darkening streets beneath failing daylight skies. Orange to peach, gold to yellow, blue to gray. With so many tenants moving in and out, I can't imagine anyone ever feeling lonely in there. "Hey, what's up?" Nodding heads pass in the imagined hallways of my mind. I crack my second beer and stand in the window. Even the now faded despairing facades of crack hotels and smack hotels deceive me with a promise of warmth and company up and away from the shouting sidewalks below. I always wanted to spend a few days in one of those hotels, just enough time to get a taste of the recklessness butting up against kinship, butting up against despair, butting up against hope, yea hope, just enough to get through the day or at least into the next check.

"What is it you want?" I hear Sylvia's haunt.

"Sleazy old man!" echoes his lonely and desperate steam reddened face from the gym just hours ago.

My mailbox on the sex site flashes I got mail. I open. "Ugly old lying troll, you say your forty-nine when your looking sixty-three!"

"Fuck off asshole! If it really matters that much to you, come over here and card me!" I write back. Fuck this online shit.

"What is it you want?" Have another beer.

Across the street, a young man leans his smooth naked torso out his window. I watch through the silence of my dark kitchen. He is thick, solid, not muscular but dense. Being so close he is fairly recognizable, not just a distant dark image in a yellow rectangle. Resting on his elbows in the exhaust blackened sill, he smokes. Down the street he watches the hustle of the corner, up the street he is pulled with the rush of traffic, down the street he lingers in loud boisterous laughter, up the street he is stopped by relentless car horns pounding against a jay walker with a shopping cart in tow slowly making his way through the intersection. I watch him across the way. He doesn't inhale his cigarette; he just blows rounded mouthfuls of smoke out into the scream. He finishes his cigarette flicking it five stories beneath him into the non-traffic street. With his arms stretching the window frame wide, the beautiful V of his masculine torso stands dark against the light of his room.

    Aroused, the plead of my fingertips imagine outlining the fall from his shoulders to his waist. It was just last night Darnell came home with me; we never did eat the cake I had lured him with. His body was like sinew, tight and twisted, every curve a muscle. But then he's the product of life in the streets, soup lines full of carbs and protein or maybe he might go stretches of days without food at all, just Meth and crack and cheap liquor. Tight and muscular. Last night he was dominant and confidant and durable for hours. I opened and allowed his driving desperation to take refuge in the surrender of my wide spread legs. The empty of my heart swelled thick and full in its new pounding as his and my lonely emptied into the writhing sheets and crying bed springs beneath us. After I came, satisfied with the job he had done he lay on his back and put his man on, stretching and curling his arm pillow-wide, beckoning me with the proud lift and backwards pull of his chin, comforting me there next to him, head resting upon his hard breathing chest, legs twining into his. His heart was beating fierce; his skin was damp beneath my cheek.

"Where are you now Darnell?" I wonder aloud as a drool of dark beer falls down my chin and threatens my neck. I lift the white of my wife beater to my face and wipe the trail dry.

"Gotta get a shelter bed" he explained as he dashed out at six this morning. "Them lines grow long quick." He paused and looked at me after that, waiting for an invitation to stay but I could not muster the courage to offer. I did not want to jump too quick into someone I hardly know. Another swill of dark brown beer and I can feel the flat of his belly under the glide of my hand. Rolling abs. Thundering rushes. Catching myself unaware, my hand circles beneath my t-shirt, round and round it goes like a woman caressing the babe she bears, round and round in slow lazy circles. My hand stops just below my navel and teases at the hair leading straight down to my pubes. Across the street, the man in the window suddenly realizes my presence and backs away like a cat in caution. He watches as I lift another swill of beer, my eyes remaining on him despite the lift of my chin. My hand follows the trail of hair leading deep into my boxers; his hand across the way is quick to follow.

FIVE

The evening runs thin, gray and cold and rain. Loneliness is the wind rattling the windows, the silence of the walls, the weight of the air. Two sided desire dashes dignity to the gutter. I'm not sure which falls harder, his or mine as we struggle to find our rhythm together, his thrust, my arching back, his steady on his knees, my spread of accommodation. I find my demanding voice in my pillow buried face. Darnell! Darnell! But these coarse brown hands flipping me, these fierce brown arms spreading me and this curved brown dick entering me do not belong to the side-eyed man on the train I met just the other night. This man, deep inside me, suddenly aggressive, crashes down upon me with all his weight, me on my belly barely able to breathe, his breath hard and wet in my burning ear. "Fucking cunt!" His unexpected anger pulls down on my shoulders while pushing the length of him into me deeper still. I twist my hips to pull away. "Take it bitch!" My hand is pinned to my side while my other pushes against the wall he thrusts me into. Thick calloused fingers filling my mouth silence my no. I bite down to express enough, but his thrusting hips ignore me. "NO!!" I twist again seeking escape. He captures me, moves with me, collars me, forcing himself even deeper.

"Fucking pussy boy!" The terror of me screams in my mind, get off me, get off me! I wanted it bad all night but not so hard, not so fast. I wanted it bad in my search for men online but listen to me listen to me. In my squirm I try to escape through the sheets, I know I just got to make it through. I cry my fear into the pillow. I cry stupidity because I just wanted it like Darnell delivered it the other night. That's all I wanted. I wanted it bad but this I never wanted. I wanted it bad but fuck I can't breathe. I want it still but just fucking slow down. I want it more but not so rough. The more I wrestle away the more he rages on.

"Stop!" I scream into the wet pillow cold on my face. I close my eyes; I close my eyes hard, my wish for Darnell my only capable prayer. Somewhere it ended. Somewhere between the collapse of my surrender and his quiver and groan.

I stand at the door as he stumbles into the bright of the hall. It is now I notice he is drunk. He didn't smell drunk. He didn't slur a word. Me on my belly, the room so dark, never caught a glimpse of his eyes. He doesn't say good night. He steps left, then steps right, lost in the direction of the elevator, forgotten are his steps leading him here just over an hour ago. I point a silent finger to the right. He is gone in the click of the closing door. "Don't leave." I whisper aloud and swallow back the pain. The smell of him is still on me. Cologne. Cheap cologne. I wait staring at the closed door wishing on some twist of fate he might return. Ten seconds waiting for the knock is a long slow burn. My mind spins insanity. I can make you late night eggs, and hash browns and pancakes. I'll give you aspirin to prevent the hangover, make sure you drink lots of water. I can draw the blinds so you can sleep in without the sun shocking you awake at seven. "Come back." I whisper to the black shut door. "Come back." I convince myself he never will.

    The kitchen window is cold; I lose myself in the lights of the city. Loneliness is an empty stove, a refrigerator with nothing good to eat, stale chips. I raise my arm high and slam the half eaten bag into the garbage. The rush unsettles me. I still smell him. I don't worry myself over his status, he said he was negative, he knows I am positive. Even if he was lying I hold no fear because I don't believe the market phobia of super-infections or re-infections; after twenty years I don't believe twice infected is worse than once. Shit, infected is infected; I have outlived my life expectancy twenty times over. Super infected? Fuck me! The only thing worse than this is death and when that time comes buy me a pack of Lucky Strikes and a fix of heroin. Tell me I am dying so I can live out my desires and curiosities; always wondered about the melt of heroin, always did love a cigarette with my beer. I drop my eyes to the dealers in the street below.

"Chiva" they beckon. "Chiva, chiva, chiva." Some days I am tempted. But I am far from dying they tell me; my condition is chronically managed. If only my fucking mind was chronically managed. Cum drips down my leg, I catch it with my fingers. At this point in my life, twenty years of waiting to get sick and die I don't give a fuck if the cum dripping out my ass is going to make my life shorter or not.

The open refrigerator door shocks my eyes into defensive slits. I bend and pull a cold one from the bottom shelf. More come and lube drip down my leg as I bend. Dang, he comes a gallon at a time. I crack the beer, turn on the stove light, wipe myself with a paper towel and stare into the geometry of tiles against the wall.

The censored conversation of my mind is a scatter. I stopped myself before saying "Give me a call sometime." Because I knew the fucker wouldn't. I stopped before saying "Would ya like to take a shower?" Because once he came his aim was for the door. I stopped before saying "Thanks for dropping by, I had a real nice time." Because I didn't. In the geometry of tiles I wonder why I crave aggression so much, and when is too much too much? If it is what I crave so deeply within me then why the fuck does it hurt so badly? Why the fuck does my heart race at the threat of a man, the threat of danger, the cowering of submission while fearing the pain and death leading up to it? Life ain't nothing without a rush in it and that rush better tremble my heart more than just a little. The geometry of tiles holds no answer.

In the street, open splayed coats sheltering

against the winds so flames can spark crack rocks pull my desire down six flights. I want to be amongst them, in the mix of them, in the camaraderie of unfeeling, in the pool of just for now. How tempting high seems, how close I come to abandon when the fucking is so damn good. But I know me and drugs. I know there is no shut off valve. I lift my beer to its empty and save crack for another day.

My eyes drift to the window across the way, the man in the perfect V appears again just as he had earlier, his hand down the front of his briefs, resting there, waiting for me to resume what we never finished. He had just pulled out his dick and got to stroking when the flash of my e-mail on a sex site signaled I had mail, a hook up, a man on his way. Two hours ago I moved from the window to prepare for the arrival of 'Aggressive Top'. Yet here we are, nearly midnight and the man in the window is still searching, I am still searching, how many hours is it gonna take to get off. I am tired. Worn. "If you only knew where my ass has been" I say aloud into the cold paned glass looking across the street at him. I consider going to bed and jacking off but I hate jacking off. It's like eating Chinese take-out alone, using chopsticks to shovel Kung Pao Chicken from a box into my mouth, losing my manners, sauce dripping my chin. Family style is what I want.

In the dark of the night he is full on, hard and stroking. The window frames him yellow. I wonder who else can see him; I jump and wonder who can see me. He signals me to come over with a scooping of his hand. I put my beer down and feel the rise of me, the urgency, the quickening of desire to make contact, to feel skin against skin, to feel the warmth of his blood rushing, to smell the wet of his black hairy crotch as I bury myself there. He strokes. I stroke. He turns and profiles the length of his tool, the run of his cupped hand along the shaft, the flat of his other smoothing his belly, his chest, finger tips pinching his nipple. I stroke. He scoops his hand again. I don't want to go. He's too close. That's not it. It's too late. Not that either. I'm too tired; never stopped me before. It could lead to a regular hook-up. Awkward if it doesn't work out, looking at him every morning while I make my coffee, every night while I am throwing something together for dinner. Another beer and I would be there without pause, I would pull my confidence into my boots, perhaps a Klonopin with the backwash of my beer. I practice my courage in the geometry of tiles. "I am Poz" I imagine myself saying once inside his front door. I will wait the entire minute of ten seconds before he turns me away. "I am Poz." I imagine seeing myself waiting for his response. His eyes do not meet mine; they search the carpet at his feet for lint. Poz. The word no is not necessary. Shame would turn my feet home; every step rejected again. No, he would not be the first; my feet know this path too well. He strokes. I drink my beer. He profiles. I swig the last, shut off the light above the stove. Burning eyes direct me to my bed. The tears are there but my tightened jaw holds them in.

SIX

I stand unnerved, a quarter past one, stuck between five and six in a four by four box with a twelve-pack of beer. So this is how I'm going to die, I cynic to myself with a half-ass smile as trembling begins the depth of my gut. Not so cynical. If it were one in the afternoon, traffic in and out of the building would set me free; a neighbor, a UPS man, the maintenance guys that vacuum the hall. This shit happens enough in these old elevators, this shit happens to everyone I tell myself but I don't listen to my own rationalization. Anxiety pounds my nerves, my heart rises into my throat. My white wiry hand strokes the painted plywood wall, the inside of this spontaneous coffin. I slap the wall sudden. "Hello!" The anxiety in me snaps. I turn and rattle the caged accordion gate, "Hello!" Only silence replies Someone will come along soon enough and push the call button from one of the floors and I will be saved I convince myself. I push button six with hope for a lift with the rise of my eyes; the closed door above, five feet away from freedom remains just that, five feet away. The bell for help has long been broken, the button snipped off by moving boxes or furniture. A black hole remains; I stick my finger in it. Steadily I press each button hoping to trigger something alive.

Here in this purgatory experience of a fucking elevator I got Hung and Loaded from the Internet on his way over and no bottle opener to pop a little compassion down to quiet these nerves of mine. Shit, I think aloud, "I've seen guys open beer bottles with their teeth." I shake my head knowing I don't fucking dare. If I was true Tenderloin I would carry a knife with me or a screwdriver at least but I wouldn't know what to do with one if I ever needed to. The flat of my hand hits the plywood wall again. My eyes lift to the ceiling as my hoodie falls off my head. I half expect to see one thin thread of a cable dangling my life here in a tease. Instead, the shock of interrogating fluorescent forbids my wonder. What if no one comes until the morning? "Damn!" Isn't there an escape hatch I am supposed to squeeze through? Isn't there a ladder that climbs me and my twelve-pack to the safety of the roof? See it now, old man climbing to safety in flip flops toting a twelve- pack.

I lean my ear the direction of voices growing from a distance; deep voices, masculine voices. "Hello!" Silence. "Hello!" Words are mumble, then radio voices jump the pause. Radio static, then radio voices again.

"Easy now. Easy" comes the soothing voice of a man just outside the door on six.

"Hello!" The elevator suddenly kicks and I am lifted the five feet to the door. I guess I am not going to die this way after all. "Fucking elevator." I slam my words indignantly as I pull the caged gate open. The elevator door swings wide. A blue uniform stands bold and broad shouldered against the white stucco hallway.

"It's broken."

"What's that?"

"It's broken." I try to step through the door but blue does not move. The radio on his belt blasts static. "The elevator is broken." Exasperated I try to wedge past him as he moves one step back. "I was stuck between five and six for about fifteen minutes until you guys came along." My eyes wander past his shoulder along an oatmeal blanket, black straps crisscrossing, a bright yellow framed gurney, the trembling patched face of my ninety-four-year-old neighbor, blood oozing the weave of gauze. Another blue uniform manages the other end of the gurney. "You might want to take the other elevator" I suggest as I realize me and my twelve-pack are stuck; the paramedic, the gurney the elevator door, the narrow hallway, my impatience. Hung and Loaded on his way.

"Put-me-back-in-my-chair!" The old man punishes each word. He lives alone across the hall from me, he eats, sleeps and shits in his recliner.

"Easy now, easy." The paramedics wrestle with the gurney, brakes, short jumps back and forth, wheels aligned, the pull is slow, a few steps down away from the door.

In the hall I step to the side and hold the second elevator door open; the elevators run side by side. "Damn." Blue flats his words nearly silent but audible enough for me to hear. He suddenly has a face, young, white, square, heavy brown brows, a thick neck supporting. Over his shoulder to the other blue the line of his jaw sharps, "We're gonna have to sit him up to get him in here." The four by four elevator won't take the six foot long gurney. I continue to hold the door even though the beer pulls me down the hall like an anxious dog at the end of a leash. Baby blue latex gloves are direct in their work. I cannot pull away from the gloves, their every move slaps me back to that sunshine street, black pavement, white sidewalks staggering onlookers and news reporters, ambulance red lights flashing, brown skin stripped to white Jockey underwear, baby blue latex gloves.

"Put-me-back-in-my-chair-God-Damn-it!" The ninety four year old face trembles his command. Neither blue pays him any mind as they begin to slowly lift the back of the gurney. "God-Damn-It!" The old man's rage is a trapped cat screaming. I stand holding the elevator door wanting a beer so bad, trembling as spastic as the old man.

SEVEN

Three blocks down she picks indifferently at her teeth with her long nailed pinky. The three front teeth are racked in gold. I hate her. Not for her teeth, but because she can get any man in the Tenderloin she wants. Granted many of them are paying, and some of them paying I wouldn't want. Still, she gets the dick I desire and I have to watch men watch her like men do, caught by the roll of her hips as she strolls, stumbled by her breast heavy bend when she picks a discarded cigarette butt off the sidewalk with enough of a stub to fire up again. I hate her. She straightens the butt, holds it between her fingertips and waits for a man with a flicking Bic. She smokes and strolls and all the men follow. I wish just one of those sets of eyes clung to my every move. Damn, the dick she must see.

She sizes the man up who stands at her side even

though she doesn't look at him. Her eyes are busily focused across the street minding the trade of dollars for small white balls of plastic. She sizes him up by the words he leans into her ear; she sorts through them like shuffling cards. Her street-wise mind has heard the story before, marked by her crossed-arm indifference. She doesn't even have to jump her argument, it rolls back over her shoulder at him, effortlessly, too familiar, as if her response has been well rehearsed. "Don't be askin' me fo no favors."

"I ain't askin' fo no favors baby, I just want to spend a little time, that's all" he explains with his sorrowful hazel eyes while his long fingered wide open palms fold in the air as if the elegance of his gesture matches the elegance of his words in his mind. She hardly breathes. She stares. Arrogance lingers like cheap perfume sold behind the counter at Walgreens; gritty, like the sugar coated candy in aisle five. I hate her. Take him! Shit, that smooth caramel colored skin and those hazel eyes. Take him! Spend some time! His flirt grinds acidic in her wake. "Now baby, you know I treat you right." Laughable, she nearly smiles, rolls her eyes down the street with the next wave of crumpled dollar bills looking to buy those small white balls of plastic. She steps away. He realizes the battle is lost, throws both arms in the air at her, takes a few long strides and stands turned away and dejected, hands on hips. Full aware my lingering there, she steps to the curb at my side.

"Whatcha ya up for papa?" Now I hate her more. Don't call me papa, bitch. I wish it was he who was hitting me up with those words. I shake my head, look over my shoulder to catch one last glimpse before I move on. He watches her hustle. "That can be arranged" she states flatly.

"Hey mama . . ." A stray male voice passes. She barely turns, barely smiles, barely nods. "Dang . . ." His voice trails into a mumble. I can tell his eyes are on her ass. She pays him no mind because it must happen every five minutes in her life. "That's a whole lotta woman right there." I hear the loiter in his voice. I hate her.

"Ya want some of that?" Her head points his direction. I feel her eyes on me. Get her, pimping him out like this. I turn into her and politely smile and shake my head no. The light turns green, I step to leave. "I know fo sure that its soooome gooood dick." She throws after me. Oh I bet it is. But it's only good if he is wanting the hole he is dicking.

Midway up the block, ole hazel eyes matches my stride. That bitch sent him after me. I hate her. "What's up papa?" I turn and steal his eyes for a minute, the full of his lips, the stretch of his jaw line. We stop aside a bus shelter.

"Not much." I smile quick at the hustle I fall into. He smiles knowing.

"Ya lookin'?" He bends into me. Stands just inches away.

"For what?"

"I dunno, you tell me."

"No. I ain't looking."

"I got what you might like."

"And what is that?"

"Eleven." I stop and look into him.

"And what do ya plan on doin' with that?"

"Anything you want." His hazel eyes go wide with the lift of his brow.

"I don't pay."

"I gotta make a dollar."

"Oh well then." I smile and turn to leave.

"When you get tired of that hand of yours, you come find me." He challenges me with a high lift of his chin. His eyes follow the strength of his nose, hand pulling on his crotch. I love it when men look down on me as if they want me to beg for it. "I know you want it." Punching his chin into the air he disappears into the mix of disembarking passengers from a bus at the curb.

"Who's that?' The voice is at my side. I spin and swallow hard in the excitement of sudden recognition.

"Hey Darnell."

"Who's that?"

"Oh some hustle. I don't know." Darnell's eyes follow hazel eyes backing down the street. His jaw tightens. The palm of his hand lays flat on my back as we move along. His finger tips press in as if giving direction. I am his possession even though we just met the other night. I like this for a minute. He looks over his shoulder repeatedly.

"Them hustlers prey on low self esteem." He drills his stare into me. "They smell it blocks away." Matching his stare. Do you smell mine? I want to ask. I let it go. I hardly know Mr. Darnell at all.

"Hey, what's your last name?"

"Wright. Named after granddaddy Wright." We walk in silence.

I press my face into his chest as the elevator lifts; hide in his layers of jacket, hoodie and t-shirts. He smells of the street; the cool of the wind down O'Farrell, the exhaust of traffic in blurring rushes, the oil of pavement, the cold and gray of cement. I catch the ammonia they wash the streets with twice a week, large tankers driving the center lane with flashing lights spraying hard fast water either side, washing the gutters clean of human waste, piss, and skinny syringes. It all rushes downhill, to wherever downhill ends. I smell fried chicken from the corner store where it sits in piles in a glass case for days on end, sometimes not resembling chicken at all, not a thigh, nor a wing, nor a leg simply cause the coating is so thick and disfigured. The heat lamps are too hot, the edges get burnt. I smell the Indian curries, bitter at first bite; the rotting pears from the fruit stand at the corner. His fingertips lift my chin to his face. His hands smell of spare change, cigar smoke and the warm of his pockets. My open mouth eats his world from the empty of his palm.

"Don't let them hustlers play you baby. Don't let no-body play you."

EIGHT

I love feeding a man. I smell his appetite through his skin, know his cravings through his moan. A man tastes of carbs and proteins and sugar; pasty starch, oily flesh, fatty sweet. In the ripe of his armpits and damp of his crotch I can bury my recipe bearing mind and come up half an hour later knowing what's for dinner. Gotta keep my man strong, gotta keep my man healthy, gotta convince him of the good thing he's found. If he is aggressive I will feed him steak; passionate, I will feed him fish; aloof, I will smother his chicken in gravy or heavy cream sauce; if he is shy, paper thin slices of ham or salami on the side. My intention is clear; if I feed him good he'll come back for more. I hope. Just last week I tumbled out of bed at five in the morning after a guy named William gave me some good dicking. Met him just standing there outside my building. A few glasses of wine and he was mine. Fucked me all night and again at dawn. That's when it's best, that's when my shit works without Viagra or Cialis or that horny goat weed I buy at the health food store. It makes me sad to think I have to take anything at all. Shit. I'm only forty-nine. Forty-nine and a half dead dick. I saw a psychiatrist about a year ago who pronounced my dick should be dead.

"So you're depressed." Pen in hand, pad on knee.

"Yea."

"Sleep a lot?"

"Yea."

"Eat much?"

"No." He notes.

"Sex?"

"What about it?"

He looks at me. "Do you have a sex drive?"

"Yea." He notes.

"Then you're not that depressed."

"Oh I am depressed."

He looks at his pad. "No Mr. Hill, you're not that depressed. Depression makes you not want to have sex" he notes.

"LOOK! I just want to feel good!" He notes, looks at me. "I just want to feel something!" He shakes his head and notes.

Maybe now I am depressed. I bought one hundred pills of Viagra online; they'll be delivered in two weeks. I'm told it won't help matters if I really am depressed. "The erection isn't the issue" my doc said. "It's desire." Shit. I take nothing with Darnell; I am hard as soon as I lay eyes on him. With guys like William, Anthony, or Mark it doesn't matter, they don't give a shit if my dick is hard or not. It's the warm, wet hole they're after. "Maybe it's just too much sex" my doc suggested. I shrug my shoulders. I count six men in four days.

It was five in the morning, black coffee steaming in my hand, gray fog of the city drifting through the kitchen blinds, garbage trucks whining the lift and dump of trash cans in the street below. I made biscuits and gravy from scratch. Sifted flour, cut lard, browned roux. Thick and comfort lingered heavy in the air; the empty of hungry shouts hollow in my belly. I thought this William or whoever he is sleeping in my bed might like that; a thick hearty breakfast for the dense powerful man who pounded my ass till near midnight and again at 4:00 AM. He stirred in his morning sleep, a mass of man under my sheets and blankets, stretching in his comfort, holding tightly like a child to the warmth found there. I nuzzled my face into his, pressed into the pillow trying to wake him with a little loving nudge. He turned quickly away, mumbling something about he can't stand morning breath. Well you didn't mind it an hour ago! I was tempted. I pull away. "Breakfast is ready."

At the table naked William sat on his stool eating pork chops and eggs and grits and biscuits and gravy with a side of warmed apple sauce. He didn't talk, just shoveled it in. Will he call? Probably not. When he left he couldn't even remember my name. He managed to mumble thanks.

Water boils. For a minute I forget what I am doing with it. Rice. Darnell likes rice. "I believe it is genetic, my craving for rice that is." He stares at me wide eyed, not even seeing me. I wonder if he is about to drop into one of those stares of his that carry him out of the room. It happens often. I pour the rice into the pot, bubbling froth rises to the top. "I have Asian blood ya know, my mama's side, she's half Native American." I look at him wondering the connection; he catches the tone of my expression. "They came from the north, the Asians did, across Alaska, down through Canada and settled here in America. I remember bein' schooled that in Texas." He stares. "That's why I like rice. Rice and fish. I'm part Asian." I step to the sink, his stare remains at the stove as if waiting for the rice to finish so he can eat. He wets his lips with his tongue and swallows deeply. The dishes in the sink are crusty with egg from breakfast. Should have given them a rinse, let them soak until after dinner.

"Are you hungry?" I turn; he is gone in a swift of silence. I stare into the empty of his absence and wonder. Who is this child in a man's body grown? Child. Child-like. So alone in the world. Who is this man who once stood recounting his elementary school lessons in the kitchen to make his mama proud, standing in the kitchen waiting for his dinner, growing faster than she can keep up? How did her heart break when she discovered him gone staring like he does? Gone staring and waiting for dinner. Did she shake his shoulders hard to bring him back? Did she slap him? She didn't buy she was part Asian, I bet. Go on now, time to wash up, I hear her say. He never got to claim his pride for what he learned at school. I know that feeling all too well, shouting epiphanies into a dulled, fast world.

I listen to sounds from the other room, trying to identify a rustle of fabric. In the spin of my mind I hear myself say trust, just trust and no harm shall come. Sounds Catholic. The blade I use for slicing lemons is too dull; I trade it for a serrated edge. I pause between slices to listen. The bathroom door just across from the kitchen closes without my knowing he ever went in. His stealth is honed for survival. I'll learn to listen for his breath, learn to look for his shadow, notice floorboards creaking in the night.

Darnell runs a bath. I pick up the trail of his clothes leading from the bed to the hall to the bathroom. The same clothes he was wearing when I met him the other night. The weight I have gathered tempts me to wash them, dirty hoodie and t-shirts are heavy, oily and grimy jeans heavier still. Clean is always light and weightless. If I wash them then I will have to empty his pockets and mess with his personals, not right without asking first. Let him tend to that. Ask him if he wants his things washed. Peeking into his back pocket his wallet is inches thick with folded papers shoved in haphazardly. Old bus transfers, small newspaper clippings and receipts poke out the edge. How does he sit on that thing? His mismatched socks are stiff and soiled, one green one blue and they smell acidic, the compost of miles and sweat aimlessly wandered. His white Jockey underwear are gray and lifeless, no longer support, just a barrier between his smooth brown skin and layers of protection. I can offer socks but do men wear other men's underwear? I wrap his socks in a plastic bag. I don't want to offend him but I can't stand the smell. I place a clean pair on top of his shoes.

Twenty minutes pass, maybe half an hour. Water runs behind the shut door. My bath tub is deep but how deep I wonder. I wash zucchini in the sink, the stroking of the green causing me to look out my window, check on the man across the way. The windows are dark, not home from work I guess. "But if you look at the genetics of African Americans . . ." I turn to the closed bathroom door. Darnell's voice is drowned by the rush of water still filling the tub. I pause before I step, wonder if he meant for me to hear him. ". . . and drug cartels are hip to that shit . . ." The water is turned off. He splashes.

"Hey Darnell. You find everything?" The door is warm to my ear.

"I'm cool."

"We'll eat in about fifteen. Alright?"

"That's cool." Water splashes.

Talking through a closed door in my own house, unsettling.

NINE

    Outside my studio window pigeons fly in flocks like fish swim in schools. Their wings flap, flap, flap as they leap from the ledge of the roof one floor up, I can hear wings beating against the air after they leap, then they turn sharp right and sail through the canyon between my building and the complex across the street, the canyon of swift air streams lifting them up, up, up. I watch them and wonder if they ever were nervous to leap and dive, I watch and wonder which pigeon leaps first, which makes the decision to leap, which makes the decision to turn right then left, which makes the decision to return to the roof ledge one flight up from my studio window. Which pigeon makes the decision with barely a sound conveyed, and how do the pigeons fly in flocks, the same grace as fish in the sea?

"I got a surprise for you." The soft of his big brown eyes smile as his cheek glides slowly over mine, lips brush their way to my ear, bite the lobe, down my neck, bite again, up to my ear. Just above silent he invites, "I wanna take ya to Christmas Eve dinner." He pulls my hips tight to his; his hand moves to the small of my back and sways me slow to the blues of Angie Stone's 'No More Rain in This Cloud.'

"Hey man, you don't need to do all that." I pull an inch away.

"But I wanna, you're good to me, I wanna be good to you. That's what makes the two of us, you and me, all the better. Ya feel me?"

My eyes close in a burn. So sweet. So fuckin' sweet. Every day these past few weeks borrowing quarters for cigarettes, tonight asking me to Christmas Eve dinner. Where did he get the money and why is he spending it on me? "What did ya have in mind?" Names of restaurants jump. Something affordable. Candlelight. Quiet table. "What will be open?"

"Oh baby, I already got these tickets ya see, for a real nice dinner." His voice lifts. "Entertainment! Food! Drinks! They're blowin' it out!" He beams in excitement.

"Dang!" Curious spins me. "Some special event then?"

"Special is right! It's Christmas Eve at the War Memorial Building." The back of his shining bald head points with a jerk in the direction. His smile wide and white.

"Dinner at the War Memorial?" Images of the large gray cement building in the Civic Center just behind City Hall doesn't make sense. I had been to many a meeting there as well as in City Hall itself; teams of us from homeless service-providing agencies advocated on behalf of the rights of homeless people, arguing against city budget cuts, demanding increased services for mental health and HIV-positive clients. Memories begin to stab my mind; memories pulling me out of this embrace, pulling me back to the streets of confusion: blood, sirens, screams, handcuffs, brown skinned cheeks and foreheads dusty from the sidewalk. A single brown tear runs a dark line through it. Delores racing in circles with her mouth covered by both her hands hysterical in her NOOOOOO! I grab Darnell tighter as the memory of her scream collapses my knees. Not now! I shout without words. Not now! The silent screech echoes my mind. I shake my head if just to clear it, scatter the thoughts. I pull myself back from those memories, back into Darnell's big brown eyes and the palm of his hand splaying my back. I stare into Darnell to not lose this moment, to not allow my mind to trap me into what I try to forget daily.

"Yea baby, Beach Blanket Babylon will be performing." Darnell's eyes lift into the spotlight of his hope, he shifts his shoulders, left then right as if busting a move.

My smile pulls me back. My lips part as I push the words shakily, "Who puts on a dinner at the War Memorial?" I spin imaginary catering companies passing hors d'oeurves and champagne on trays carried by smiling stiff white shirts, red lipstick mouths wording inaudible invitations, "Crostini with olive tapenade, porcini stuffed mushrooms, balsamic glazed roasted figs, you're welcome." Campy big-hatted Beach Blanket of Babylon costumes parading in song.

"AIDS Housing Alliance and other Housing organizations. They're gonna have everything baby, turkey, stuffing, green beans, cranberries, salad, dessert . . . everything. They'll be blowin' it out! I just hope we get more than one helpin'." The palm of his hand circles his belly. "I love turkey and some extra green beans with them crispy onions on top."

His arms wraps around me. He makes his way through the dinner line again and again and again. A boy at Christmas with eyes bigger than the meal ticket in his wallet. I manage a smile; hide my face in the curve of his neck, heat rising from his skin a warm compress against the sting of my cold arrogant tears. Images of a romantic dinner, he and me, doused like candles as a glamorized soup line emerges, Tenderloin faces, noisy tables, lukewarm food slopped onto paper plates, never enough gravy. The thought of being pity-eyed by the advocates I used to work with standing there serving up the portions kicks me in the balls, them knowing I am too fucked up to work because my nerves just can't stand being in that office ever again, can't stand the thought of walking down that terrible street, can't stand the cringe of loud shouting voices, can't stand the shame of them seeing me this way, not being strong enough, not now, not then.

"Hey man, how ya doing?" I can hear them ask. A question repeating in my head over and again even when they are not standing before me asking it. A question not answerable because tears choke my words and I have no fucking idea of how I am doing because normal is beyond my recall to compare. "Fine." I will mumble and turn away. Maynard is fucking dead and Grayson sits happily dressed in orange in jail eating his version of fucking Christmas dinner. "Fine." I will continue. "More gravy please."

    Darnell's arms wrap me, sway me, breathe me. "I know you're used to better baby." He stumbles and scrambles for his words; I feel his unsteady, his caution abrupt. "But, if ya wanna settle for a little less, I mean, if ya wanna, I would like to date ya." He presses the back of my head harder into his shoulder with the palm of his warm hand not allowing me to pull back and look at him. Safe from rejection, safe from seeing my eyes that says it all, safe from pain on the eve of Christmas Eve. As he continued his words sped. "I'll get a job here soon enough baby. I'll treat ya the best I can. Ya know baby, I like you, I wanna be your boy friend and shit. Take ya on vacation somewhere. Trains. I like trains." My cheeks run wet, my breath stopped in my chest. No one has ever wanted me so much, so hard. Darnell's eyes go drifting on some train ride down the grains of the hardwood floorboards beneath our feet. He stares for nearly a minute before he speaks again. "They watched me once in videos" he mumbles with a turn of his head as if hearing far away. "They put it on the Internet." My eyes shut a little tighter as Angie Stone's R&B lyrics sing my heart to a place beyond reason, beyond the slip and slide of his nonsensical words.

    My sunshine has come
    And I am all cried out
    There's no more rain in this cloud

I rock this man gently, sing soft in his ear as his eyes run wet and his hard breath flares his nostrils. I wonder what is his pain.

TEN

Across the street in the alley he stands, black is his jacket, his pants, his military boots laced high his shin, sunglasses shards of white reflections piercing my notice of his notice of me, a long black bag throws his shoulder, his brown skin sweats in the sun. Monday morning Ninth Street, South of Market outside my office; rush hour traffic blurs four lanes between us; brown UPS trucks, yellow taxis, angry horns, the long narrow familiar of the tension between me and him, my sudden quiet tremble for help. In the next wave of box moving vans he disappears. Down the alley, down the street, into the parking garage I am not for certain. Anger lingers the air or is it just my imagination. I tremble unlocking the office door.

    I spend the day watching over my shoulder, cautious of sound and movement; a shout across the room from one case manager to another, the stagger of swearing clients, the squeal of impatient car tires outside, the ringing of my phone. I walk home backwards, constant glances over my shoulders, waiting for Grayson to appear again.

 A year and a half ago is today; today is lost in the flash of then. Grayson is there but he isn't. The sidewalk across the street is empty but there he stands. I walk but I don't feel my feet. His voice comes louder than traffic. "YOU'RE THE FUCKING PROBLEM HERE! NOT ME!" How did I get to the corner of Hyde and Ellis? What the hell am I doing here anyway? I walk down Hyde looking back, waiting for him to reappear. He is nowhere to be seen.

  The Chinese market on Ellis sells rice cheap, rice for Darnell, easy to make, two to one, I don't have to think. I want a rice cooker so I can think even less but cooking in aluminum isn't good for you. I can't remember why. They sell broken rice even cheaper than regular rice. What is broken rice? Or better yet, how does rice get broken? Plastic woven bags line the shelves. Ten varieties of rice it seems including broken rice. All I want is plain rice. "Excuse me." I wave the attention of the Chinese merchant. "Excuse me. Is Jasmine rice regular rice?" Non-expression stares at me like I am a fucking idiot asking the fucking obvious. Wrinkles dart the bridge of his nose. I grab Jasmine rice. I'll take my chances.

  Back on the street Grayson is there, just as he was on Monday; waiting again for me to arrive to work this Tuesday morning. I throw the bag of rice over my opposite shoulder so I can watch him watching me.

Each step of mine he remains unmoved, arms crossed in his waiting.

I was beaten last night as I was falling asleep, his angry fists pounding punches into my face, bones crackling. His military boots kicked my balls. I saw pain. It was blue. He shouted unceasingly. "Fire my ass! Fire my ass! You racist mother fucker!" I finally fell asleep with one eye open. I awoke in a knot of sheets.

Grayson stands the same posture, wearing the same clothes, unmoved by my attention of him. He wants to be seen. He wants to scare the shit out of me. He wants me to lose my mind before he kills me. I watch for traffic at the corner, left and then right and then he is gone. I swing side to side with the rice on my shoulder. I nearly lose my balance. My eyes dart searching.

"I need help!" I stress into the receiver of the phone.

"Sorry Daniel, there is nothing we can do." The pause in the phone line is the wait before the kill. "The police won't do anything about people hanging out on the street, no proof of stalking, no use in calling." My supervisor's tone cares but doesn't care. "Were the locks changed after he was fired?" I hang up knowing I am on my own.

I walk along Ellis balancing the rice, weaving between round Latinas and strollers, electric wheelchairs without speed limits, dogs on leashes. The bag molds itself over my shoulder, gets heavier every few steps. Ten pounds seems like fifty. Maybe broken rice is lighter. Grayson steps the opposite side of the alley and hides from my view. I can't see him but I know he is there. I hold my steady gaze; I won't lose sight of him today like I did yesterday. He peeks his head around the corner of the building. His back is flat against it. He acts like a cop on some television show. I wonder if he has a gun. A gun? I jump into a doorway panicking. The office! The office! Get in the office! With my one free hand I can't find my keys to get into my office. I dig in my pockets. I can't find my keys! This bag of rice is too fucking heavy. Drop the fucking bag! Drop the fucking bag! The bag hits the cement with a thud. On the corner of Ellis and Hyde my hands dig my pockets frantically. Get in and call the police. "Call the police! Call the police!" A white old man stares at me under bushy eyebrows, a round face, a pouty lower lip, thick salt and pepper hair. The odd of him causes me to scan the doorway. The Ben Hur Apartments, Roman Chariots the wall decor. This is not my office. The street stinks of exhaust, a parked car revs its engine in front of me. Grayson is nowhere to be seen. A tall lanky street sweeper walks by in his blue coveralls, clear round safety glasses, got his head set on, pumping his groove as he pauses in his sweeping. Ninth Street ain't Ninth Street at all. The alley is a space between buildings. My eyes walk up the slow hill of Hyde and then fall back to my feet, the ten pound bag waiting to go home.

ELEVEN

Tea lights burn across my altar. My mind leaps like their flicker before me, then rests in a steady stretch of flame. I take to counting my breaths, one, two, three, then my mind goes wandering again. The cycle repeats itself over and over, each time I lose my count I notice impatience, I usually reach ten before beginning again but this morning my mind jumps and jumps. I remind myself the practice is simply coming back to my breath, not how high I can count with an unwavering mind. Still, twenty minutes into my meditation I give up. Rambling thoughts have made breakfast and lunch and gone to the gym and I haven't even left the cushion. My knees come up under my chin as I wrap my arms around them under the itch of my wool blanket. I stare into the burning tea light flames, their dance reflects off the porcelain statue of Quan Yin, the Goddess of compassion. I sit in the cold of the morning air staring blankly into the flames until the candle snuffer douses the last. Smoke curls around the dense image of the brass Buddha.

TWELVE

His want hits the corner before he does; his want, larger than the do-ragged, gold chained, baggy pants sharp of him arrives a good thirty seconds before his glide comes into view. The warm tremble in the crisp cold air alerts me of his coming, chill bumps dancing on my skin agree, the hard swallow in my throat confirms, his want comes marching full on strong. When he steps up curbside across the street, my mouth airs open and wordless, my keen slaps me unnerving, an open palm on my bare ass while getting fucked telling me to relax, relax, let me get in there.
    Smooth is his prowess behind the pitch dark tint of his shades while the black silk do-rag sliding down the back of his head, tied in a knot to hold tight and steady takes me rushing in a chase of anxiety, a breathless sharp of fear. Death and orgasm are just

a heartbeat difference and all too familiar as I ride this shaking nerve into the pause between the two. Ghetto reads the lust of danger. I burn in the flush of heat rushing my December chilled face, I flinch in the gratifying sting of fingertips pinching my nipples and making them hard even though I stand alone fully dressed on the opposite corner from him, nipples hard and erect, pointing me, leading me, as one bold pivot faces me his coming direction.

    I race along the quickened passion running my heart on two legs, four legs, sixteen legs and pumping. Faster and faster still knowing the green light will carry his fine ass into my waiting patience, into my lair of desire. His want screams over the traffic, louder than the sirens, pounding in repetition like a relentless car alarm; a scream too familiar, knowing soon enough I'll be the wanted and I'll be the one screaming for more, to slow down, go easy, push it deeper and deeper still.

    "I get a rush from it."
    "From having sex . . ."
    I am paused by his assumption. "Before sex." I gaze into the flipping flash cards of memories. "Like when I hear their voices on the phone before I say anything, or when they stop on the street after I have stared them down." I feel him watching me as my eyes fall in renewed excitement to my hands. A glimpse of the rush comes. "As soon as I hear their breath on the receiver or the depth of their voices leaning into me I am chilled to being frozen dumb." You got a place to go? I'll be there in twenty. What's your address?

Yea, I'm looking to get into something, what about you? The cards flash. I shiver thinking about it. Velvet voices. Deep engines turning. Confidence pushing. Not a face to their words, not a name I recall, lips, just full moving lips. Lips I want to hear call to me, lips I want to hear moan.

"What is the thrill Daniel?" I hear his pen slide over the lines of his long yellow legal pad balanced on one knee. Dr. James, legs spread in the therapist posture of importance, feet planted flat, bracing for the good stuff. The meat. The blood juicy rare. I like his side burns.

"Thrill?" I never considered it a thrill. I want to pull away from his question. My eyes fall to his crotch and wonder how big his dick is. "Or is it fear?" I roll my eyes away. Can't fantasize my fucking therapist but I do anyway. Loosen his tie.

"Are you afraid Daniel?"

My word slides. "Sometimes . . ."

"What are you afraid of?"

"Getting hurt." My matter of fact stops us both.

"Why do you think getting hurt gives you a thrill?"

"I said it's not a thrill." My eyes meet his. Ashamed I feel. "Thrills are for roller coasters." My words spit at him. His brown eyes say tell me more. "A roller coaster is safe. You got that padded harness. You know the ride is only going to last a few minutes or so. People get on, people get off . . ."

"Do you feel safe?"

"When?"

"When one of these guys comes over. Or even before they come over . . ."

I pause and consider safe, consider faces of men I can recall. "Sometimes not . . ." My hands tighten around each other; fingers are bones knotting onto each other. "Sometimes I guess I feel I am in danger because I am trapped, because I might get ripped off, get hurt . . ." I shift on the leather couch. I try to right myself. I always slip down low in the couch. No butt to hold me up. I feel trapped right now I realize; his sternness, this line of questioning. I consider the width of his shoulders, the thick of his chest beneath his pockets; I wonder what he smells like around his neck, cologne or after shave or the sweat of man. Unbutton his top collar, one by one move down the line of white pearls. "But sometimes it's exciting . . ." His smooth brown muscular chest will reveal solid his heart, fierce his knowing.

"Let's go back to feeling scared. What happens when you feel trapped?"

I don't want to go back to feeling scared, my little fantasy was finally making me feel good. "I begin to fall inside myself." His frown of not getting what I say hovers between us. His eyes search. "It's like I know what's coming and I can't get away and I can't stop myself from bringing it on, encouraging it, wanting it . . ." I drift. His face is lost in the perpendicular lines of shelved books against the wall behind him. "But I fall into this place where nothing matters and I don't give a fuck." The perpendicular lines are watery and blurred now. Lined colors fading into one another, running down over his shoulders it seems. "Not-feeling. Not-knowing. Not-aware of him or me." The burn of my eyelids blinks me awake. "But feeling pain . . .

when I do . . . is fine because it is something." Flash cards. Bitch take that dick! Fucker open that ass! Slap goes his hand. His palm pins my ankles over my head. "And . . . I know . . . he wants me. I know it. He wants me." My words are sobs choking that place between us. "I will take care of him. That's what I do . . . take care of him." I can't make out his face for the tears but I know he looks at me with pity. Shame is cold. I wipe my tears and wonder, where was I? Pulling his shirt tails from the depth of his slacks. "Sometimes it's exciting . . ."

Dr. James pauses. "Sometimes it's trying to relive a traumatic experience in hopes of a better outcome."

THIRTEEN

I set my alarms, two of them, obsessive I am. One stares me down at my bedside the other across the room on my desk; if the first does not rouse me the second will. The weight of blankets settles; fleeting security does not rest my eyes any easier. I stare into the blue of the room, fingers clinging to the mesh beneath my chin. I don't want to let go. My face buries under warmth, nests there, a drift is the moment dissipating with a damp exhale.

Waiting for sleep. The steady pace of thoughts wearies me; work in the morning, Grayson on the street, grocery shopping, fruit, eggs, cheese, granola; laundry piles, need bleach, an overdue call to my father, call him next Sunday, not right after church but not after four; he eats dinner, movies, then bed. Fuck it I'll call on Saturday. Fuck! I cannot sleep. Saturday, it's going to rain.

Night sounds are relentless; I pick apart shouts from the street, try to pull away from conflict; afraid of silence in between, I am drawn back in. My head peeks from the covers to pull the world closer. High pitched voices, angry words punching, anxiety is a low growl of a man, despair is hearing her weep. Accusations sling between the shout high and the shout low, guttural groans of disagreement drop the argument to its knees, voices move away along the sidewalk, distancing, finally lost around the corner. My body lies rigid.

Empty bottles escape recyclers digging trash bins, bottles tumble downhill capturing the echo of Leavenworth, ting-ting, ting-ting they go. Aluminum cans crush beneath stomping feet, crackle, smash, metal against metal. Sirens stop a block or so away followed by more sirens; what's going on out there, tempted to go to the window. Up on my elbow I wonder if shouts are connected to sirens. Is she in pain? Did he hurt her? The 27 Bryant bus stops across the street voicing its recorded destination, "27 Bryant, Van Ness and Jackson."

Sleep settles in, I am drunk with it, awake for a moment, the room is blurred, my eyes close under the weight of heavy lids but lift again to capture an unfinished thought; buy bleach and softener. Sleep. At last sleep, pierced by a siren whining, perhaps the same siren as earlier, perhaps not. Grayson is in my office, the opposite side of my desk; his hands are huge, eyes springing from their sockets. The sirens pitch loud and louder still. He has me cornered, fists hammering the desk top. "LIES . . .! His words lost to the sirens. "LIES . . .! LIES . . .! LIES . . .!" His eyes are bloodshot, raging, fists throwing punches, sirens screaming, me curling in, curling in, shrinking beneath the desk only to be found by his fury. My arms go up in defense, fists so huge there is no escape. Red lights flash; sirens go round and round, fists of rage are now pointing fingers, pointing fingers jabbing into me. His eyes jump from their sockets, "YOU ARE THE FUCKING PROBLEM MR. HILL! YOU ARE THE FUCKING PROBLEM, NOT ME! NOT ME! NOT ME!" The sirens will not stop, the room is red, walls dripping red, carpet soaked in red, my hands defensive fists of red. "YOU'RE THE WORST FUCKING SUPERVISOR I HAVE EVER WORKED FOR!"

    I jump into the blur of awake; blink red to white, flashes of lights scatter through my windows. I am awake. I know I am awake. I throw the covers off, step to the window. Radio voices scratch the cold night air. My heart shakes, hands tremble. It is so damn cold. Fuck! Why is it so damn cold? Out the window I glare. What the fuck is going on? As my eyes fall into the street, fire engines angle and line the far lane of Leavenworth, long white hoses stretch from trucks up the front steps of the building across the street. Firefighters in heavy gear stand the sidewalk. Anxiety ended the last siren ago. If there was an emergency it is over now. I turn from the windows and return to bed, jumping into the evaporating warmth of my sheets. Still, I am shaking. I cling to the blankets and pillows like never letting go.

    My eyes open slowly, sleepily into the blue dawn

filling my room. Blue dawn. "Fuck!" I realize I have overslept. "What the fuck? Overslept?" I reach for the alarm at my bedside set to wake at 5:00 a.m., yet the clock reads 6:00 straight up. I jump and check the second alarm. What the hell happened? My eyes spin the room, my fingers cutting through the thick of my hair. Am I awake? What the fuck happened? I don't know how to begin. I can't figure out what time I have lost and what the fuck I normally do in that time. Routine is shattered glass, me trying to assemble razor sharp pieces, every jagged edge cutting, not fitting, the fucking impatience of it all.

Panic. Too late to pack lunch, too late to drink coffee or have breakfast. Time for a quick shower, out the door I go. Fuck the shower just go to the gym, work out, shower there, get some breakfast along the way. Time for coffee? Where is my gym bag? What should I wear? Jeans, thermal, T-shirt. Which T-shirt? Don't forget a belt. I stumble through decision, fall into action, pause in between and doubt what I do. My body moves, mind trying to blink awake. Fuck I need a goddamn cup of coffee to get my ass moving. Grayson's image flashes. Red. Paused in thought my hands slow the packing of clothes. Flashes of red. I slide my belt through the loops. Flashes of Grayson. I slip on my boots.

Through the gate of my building the street unfolds, daylight steeping cautious like tea. I leap from my stoop into the street; the soles of my boots slap against the sidewalk. I am stopped. The world stops. The air is cool and fresh. The bus passing on the street glides without sound, the man who walks around me does not disturb the still place I find myself in. A delivery truck across the street idles in silence, the dark shadow of the driver blowing blue cigarette smoke out the window. I am not moved to step into my stride. My eyes rest in the gray of the street, the lighter gray of the sidewalk. My short breath secures the calm.

Pushing out of my trance I head through the sun-glimpsed morning. Colors breathe as I pass. The Cadillac Hotel, turquoise and gold trim appear clean, new, despite aging peels of paint. The yellow of a school bus is canary. Orange traffic pylons bold themselves in the shadows of dawn. White lines designating crosswalks stretch across Eddy Street; the twelve steps I take to pass through those lines are strong and confident, safe and assured.

The corner at Leavenworth and Turk stands innocent; vacant of dealers and addicts, the hustle of last night swept away by boisterous hydraulic sweepers, hardly anyone moves through the streets. A young man passes hiding under his hoodie, arms swing at his side, oars pushing through water; face fixed to the ground, his hand raises, finger plugs one nostril, he blows snot, shakes his hand in the air, wipes it in his black pants. I can't hear his steps in the fresh of his gleaming sneakers. The silence of Grayson stalking me the week before flashes clear and is gone, flashes again at the thought of him and is gone as quickly. My stride is not interrupted.

Stores stand shut, iron gates spread across dark windows and doors. Chains, padlocks wrap heavy through handles, once, twice, three times through.

Safety, protection, guarded I think as I go. The Vietnamese Karaoke bar hides behind sheets of plywood, behind a folding iron fence. Blue recycling bins stand full on the curb, green Heineken bottles from the night before. Even the smell of beer this early does not turn me sour.

The day is sharp, alive. The world breathes around me as I watch the S of the cars jogging Seventh Street to McAllister to Leavenworth. I have never seen them as elegant, was never moved by their rush, only annoyed by their impatience, noise and push. They pass without interruption heading up the Leavenworth hill. The day is different; the calm in me is deep even though I see red.

I shade my eyes the corner of Ninth and Howard, a block from work yet a corner I do not know. Unease blurs the slow minutes, the past two hours, anxiety has risen like the sun blazing now. I rode a bus I never take, got breakfast from a café I've never been to, glimpsed not a familiar morning commute face. I walk with the flow of traffic rather than against it, the rev of a truck engine spins me around. My hand trembles down the side of my face, fingers falling to cover my mouth. My eye set on Starbucks, I want a cup of coffee. Impatience. The emptiness of my stomach, cry of hunger, need for caffeine, disorientation of time; I wonder if I am early, I know I could be late. My hand clenches a bag with breakfast, a croissant sandwich, fruit salad. Is the sandwich still warm? I moan the thought, cold eggs on a soggy croissant. I doubt my stomach will let me eat even crying as it is. Disquiet thunders from my bones; irritation, nerves to quiver. I turn my face into the heat of the sun. Red. I close my eyes. I breathe deep, gym soap. I hate the smell. I breathe again; Starbuck's across the street catches the wind.

    Traffic pushes heavy, busier than normal, louder than I recall. Am I late? I can't be late. I want to sit down. My legs are weak, they shake. I ran the treadmill at the gym for an hour; ran from Grayson, the dream the night before, the stalking the previous week, the unleashed anger towards me a year and a half ago. I ran and didn't even know I ran for so long; could have kept fucking running; never did that before, lost I ran in fear. My knees in their unsteady want to bend.

    I wait on the light, eyes lost in the asphalt before me. The distance to the other side beyond my ability to reach. Irritation burns. Red. I see red again. What the fuck is red? Run now. Run the opposite direction, run from this fucking job, run from this fucking neighborhood, run from this angry city, just get the fuck away. The hammer of my heart more fierce now than on the treadmill. Rushes pound my ears, my hands rise to quiet them. I remember trembling in the shower, could barely hold the soap.

    The crosswalk light shouts green. How long has it been green? The keenness of early morning captures my eyes again. The world is exaggerated. Trees balloon in green. Buildings rise taller than they are, wider, thicker; rooftop edges sharp, windows reflect blue skies. I fix on the silver Chevron gas station across the street, the orange, red, and blue of Burger King streaks my sweep. The bright red sign of Andretti's Mini-Mart alarms; the forest green of Starbucks pulls me back to my craving. People pour through doors fueling the morning awake. Each person is distinct. My eyes jump from one to another looking for familiar, looking for someone I know, someone to help. Help with what? This unsettled feeling.

I think again of Grayson; my jumping eyes race along the people I see. Light still green I step cautious between lines in the crosswalk, not strong, not confident. Grayson has to be here, every fucking day last week he was here. Fear scans the gas station parking area, up ahead the sidewalk, across the street from my office under the trees, the alleyway where he ducked in, out, watching me, scaring me, the garage at the end of the block where he hid. I still see him all in black.

Sidewalk glare stretches before me decreasing distance between me and my office; attention falls upon two figures sitting outside, backs against the wall, piles of belongings stack at their sides. My hand searches for keys as their faces come into view. The homeless man who sleeps in the doorway, the man I wake up every morning. Reginald Simmons, our new hot tempered client. They pass a paper-sacked bottle between them.

"Good morning!" shouts Reginald, not waiting for response. He lifts his dirty black T-shirt, wipes his face.

"Hey! How ya doin?" the homeless man slurs. "Oh, it's you!" He laughs and turns to Reginald. "That guy..." He taps Reginald's shoulder, points my direction with his thumb. "That one there... he's my alarm clock!" He laughs deep in intoxication; sharp scent of beer hangs the air. Reginald smiles, nods, lifts the tall bottle from the homeless man's hands. I recognize the gold and burgundy label peaking through, Old English 800.

    I look across the street, into the alley. Bright sun reveals the empty place Grayson stood one week ago today. I find my keys; my hand can barely hold them. My chest is dead. I cannot swallow, I cannot breathe. I reach for the keyhole, stopped in my own trembling and wonder, 'Why is the homeless man awake and not in the door?' I step quickly away from the door. I stare at it. I am washed with distrust. Did Grayson turn in his keys when he was fired? Were the locks changed? I want to ask the two men if anyone has entered the office, but my words don't come.

    "Hey Mr. Daniels! I wanted ask you somethin'." Reginald rolls his legs to the side, readying to get up. I raise my hand, shake my head.

    "Not now Reginald, when we open up I can answer your questions."

    "That's what I wanted to ask you Mr. Daniels, when exactly do you open up?' His eyes narrow, focus just beyond the curb in slurred squint.

    "Ten o'clock, Reginald."

    "Oh, well what time is it now?"

    "Just before eight thirty, maybe eight-fifteen, I think." I turn to check the alley across the street. Empty. "Maybe eight forty-five . . ." My mouth opens to form words. The homeless man sits upright, turns to Reginald Simmons, repeats "That guy there is my alarm clock! He wakes my ass up every morning at eight-thirty!" He laughs again. Reginald hands him the bottle for another round, shakes his head. The homeless guy is up and out of the doorway to drink beer with Reginald I say to myself.

    The tremble of my hand pushes the key into the lock. I turn the deadbolt over, feel it click, push the door open, step into the cool of the office. Reaching behind me I turn the deadbolt again, it falls under its weight. Locked. I sweep the lobby with my eyes along the rows of vacant chairs, struck by the sudden still. I push into it, look into the depths to notice the unusual in any way, to catch any movement, any disturbance. My heart pounds out of my chest. Still I push myself across the short lobby, through the half door, into the Case Management office. My eyes scan for difference but the same is just the same. Each desk sits in usual order, my left, my right, each partition push-pinned with housing notices, soup line schedules, clinics and dentists, clothing and childcare. One side to the other, the same is just the same yet I push each step of mine, push against the heaviness of my heart.

    The office darkens as I go, the back of the office a long black shadow. I pause, can't swallow, hold my breath unlocking my office door, hands trembling. No lights I step into my office, stand in the light the open door casts. I cannot stay here another minute alone. Getting out repeats itself, over and over, I can think of nothing else. Get out! I lay my gym bag, shoulder pack, and breakfast croissant on the table. Get out! Backing through the door I creep, get out! I turn, the office longer than it typically appears, it lengthens as I aim for the front, get out! Shadows of two men outside the yellow blinds, my heart leaps, jumps me into a sprint for the door. I swoop upon the deadbolt, unlock it's tumble throw it open push my way into Mr. Simmons and the homeless man.

I jump from one face to the next expecting to see Grayson, turn into the morning rush of Ninth Street, brown UPS vans, blue Super Shuttle vans, buses, taxis, cars, revving motorcycles. Peet's Coffee a couple of blocks away. Sit down, drink coffee. I'll wait at Peet's until the others arrive.

Ninth Street silent, emptiness sharp cutting the bone, the cold of 'no' rushing a flesh of chill bumps head to toe, a turmoil of pain and wind and heave. I step faster, the drumbeat of my heart pumping in my ears. My eyes fix a block away, figures of men falling, tumbling, blue uniforms swarming. I race down the street towards my office, asphalt pounding, haze blinding; black and whites scream sirens in their coming, tires squeal making the corners, blue uniforms outrace me, a box red ambulance pushes its way through the swarm of cars stopped by two motorcycle cops at the end of the block. My feet are numb running, running. I know it is bad. Fuck I know it is bad.

Grayson lays on the sidewalk, the black of his clothes brown, his face dusted with gray dirt of the street. The fucker is handcuffed; his face presses into the sidewalk; small bits of gravel stick to the quiver of his lips. I stand before him. He does not see me. His eyes are closed. My rage rises; he has fucking done something but I don't know what. Rage screams and rises and tears its way through me, pulls it's temptation through me, screams at me to pull my foot back and wield hard kicks into that ugly fucking face. That ugly fucking angry face of his! Kicking! Kicking! Just pull back and kick like I have never kicked in my life.

"Dan-i-el! Dan-i-el!" Aakil's voice shatters, his familiar African-French accent peals my attention from Grayson's body, the tremble in his voice chills me to knowing something horrible happened. I turn to Aakil but he is not there. Police dash the street, yellow police tape stretched from tree to pole to parking meter. Aakil? Where is Aakil? "Dan-i-el! Dan-i-el!" What the fuck happened? What the fuck happened? I turn again but I don't see Aakil. "Dan-i-el! Dan-i-el!"

My heart drops to the sidewalk before me; three men sit on the curb not far from where I stand. Aakil's face lifts above the other men's heads, his face dusted gray like Grayson's, does not read the radiance of him, voice does not sing his words in music, his face a dusty shell. A wide-eyed shell. Stunned, shocked, tears streaming.

I recognize each man; the homeless man, Reginald Simmons bouncing on his toes, Aakil, fixed on me, dusty gray in disbelief. "Oh my God Dan-i-el! You are alive! You are alive!" He sits on the curb holding his shoulder with his hand. Aakil's words reach through my confusion, his left hand takes mine, shakes it. "Oh my God! I thought you were in there dead Dan-i-el! Dead!"

My eyes are thrown down the sidewalk, the scream of a woman's voice. Her ring studded brown hands cover her face, boots stomp the ground. She wails deep and long and hard. I know it is Delores, my Case Manager, falling curls of her wig, gold rings, sharp crease of her perfectly pressed jeans.

Barely able to find my voice I manage "What happened Aakil? What the fuck happened?"

"He shot Maynard! He shot Maynard! Maynard is in there lying on the floor!" I pull away from Aakil and step two steps towards the office. "I thought it was you Dan-i-el. I thought it was you!" The door packed with police, a paramedic dashes out of the office, sight set on the ambulance, races through their stagger and sweeps into the vehicle. He retrieves a large plastic box, runs back through the door. I shouldn't have left. I shouldn't have left.

Chaos slaps me in the face. Maynard screams my mind. I ran. I can't believe I fucking ran. "He had a gun! Grayson had a gun pointing at me when I opened the door!" Aakil swallows hard. "I jumped him Dan-i-el! He pointed the gun at me and I jumped him!" Aakil tosses his arm in the air reenacting the siege. His tears stream, his face twists. Delores wails, a ball crouched on the sidewalk. Aakil moans, holding his shoulder. "Reginald grabbed the gun. Reginald saved us Dan-i-el!" At Aakil's side Reginald shakes, his eyes bouncing. I left Maynard! I fucking ran when I should have stayed! I left Aakil. I left Delores. I turn to Aakil, he grimaces in pain.

"I have to get to Delores." I sidestep Grayson's trembling form on the ground. Delores is back on her feet, sees me coming through scattered police.

"Oh my God!" she screams. "Oh my God!" Her arms stretch the air. "You're alive! You're alive!" She resumes stomping, her arm points through the door of the office. "I been thinking you were in there! I been thinking you been shot and dead!" She wails, wraps her arms around me. "Oh my God Daniel! Oh my God!" Her face in her hands again, head shaking, she rises with flaring eyes, "Daniel! Oh my God Daniel! I seen him headin' for the office wit dat big ole black bag. I knew it was bad Daniel! I knew it was goin' to be bad! But I was in my car! I couldn't do nothin'! I couldn't stop!" Hysterical she throws her hands down to her sides, shaking her hands, throwing her arms. "I went in dere! I went in dere when Aakil had Grayson on de groun! Guns was on de counter, all da furniture is tumbled all over da place! Blood on the walls! And den I seen him! Lyin' dere on da floor! I start screamin' Maynard to git up! Git up an kick his fuckin' ass! I screamed! Git up and kick his ass!" Her hand reaches across her mouth, eyes narrow in pain, chest heaves, tears smear wetted cheeks. "He didn't move Daniel! He didn't move!" Her eyes jump in panic, her mouth opens a silent scream, arms punch tight in the air. "I just stood dere screamin' for him to git up! And den I leaned down on him and pounded on him wit my hand! Git up Maynard! Git up! But he wouldn't budge, he wouldn't push off. He just lay dere! Dere was nothin'! He didn't move! That's when I saw the bloooood!" Delores steps back, bends and curls into herself. I move to comfort her. "I saw dat blood and I came screamin' out dat door! I came screamin' out dat door! Oh God Maynard! Oh my God Maynard!" Her wails scream into muffled sobs. "Noooo. Noooo. Noooo."

Maynard never could sit still. Even as the paramedics pull his body from our office I half expect to see his feet bouncing, see him jump up, fidget at something. I half-expect him to run with one of the five ongoing conversations we had with each other at any given time that never did find an end. They pull his near naked form through the doors, into the street. They had cut his clothes away. White Jockey underwear against the smooth of dark brown skin. Chest heaving then not heaving at all. Handsome face lost under a plastic breathing device as baby blue latex gloves push the gurney through standing police. Maynard disappears into the ambulance, red lights flashing in rhythm, red lights the rhythm of a heartbeat, red lights the repetition of a prayer barely audible from my lips. I watch the ambulance race down the long empty street.

    Black. Everything inside the squad car, black. Black seat, black carpet, black dash, black computer screen, black guns. His blonde hair led me to the car, closed the door, took me downtown to take a statement. He sits there next to me; navy uniform appears black, blonde hair yellow. He turns the key, I can't hear the engine. The cruiser glides slowly; strong, silent, sturdy. Tears rush my eyes; they burn as I hold the anger of my failure. I should have never left. I breathe deep into the tremble, breathe into my heart that skips, into the painful tight of my belly, into the anxiousness of my hands grasping, coming up empty. I look out the window to my side, feel this cop's gaze upon me. I don't want to be seen, just want to lie down, close my eyes, curl into myself and hide.

Beyond the yellow tape familiar client faces. Confusion. Concern. They want their checks; they came for their morning disbursements, they came for Maynard, Delores, Aakil. One client paces short circles, another lifts her arms in the air, exasperation twisted across her face. She shouts. The crowd of people around her ignore her. I can't hear her. The car is silent. The ride is smooth. The world is far away. I am safe, I think. Don't make me leave this feeling. Don't make me leave this car. Just let me slip into the black.

"What's your name?"

"Daniel. Daniel Hill."

"A hard way to start your week." His chin points his matter of fact words over the steering wheel.

"Yea, not how I planned . . ." I trail, unable to focus. Tears stronger than words right now, keep my mouth shut or they will fall.

"Did you know that guy?"

Silence hangs between us until I can manage, "Which guy?"

"The guy that got shot." He takes his eyes off the road to look at me.

"Yea, he was one of my staff." My words echo in the black. I close my eyes, see Maynard on the gurney. I close my eyes harder, see only black.

"That's gotta be hard." Silence drops again. My words are there but I cannot speak. I feel him watching me. He drives on. A few minutes pass. "What about the gunman?"

"What?" I turn, open my eyes to a blur.

"Did you know the gunman?" Images of Grayson on the sidewalk; I am too numb to want to kick him.

I stare my knuckled hands, Maynard on the gurney, blue latex gloves. I shouldn't have left.

"Yea. I knew him too . . ." I look out my window as colors wash into black, feel him watching me.

We make our way into city grid, traffic snarled every direction. Buses stand empty, stranded, faces in cars stare at me through the passenger window. The trail of squads carrying Delores, Reginald, the homeless man, me ignite sirens, push assertively through slow parting traffic.

"How bad was it?" I mumble, not wanting to know the answer but loud enough to get his attention.

"What's that?" He leans toward me. I feel his concern though I can't turn to face him. He cares. I want him to hold me.

"How? How bad was it? How bad was he? The shot, I mean, the shot. How bad was he shot?" I push the words, they echo between us, echo off the dashboard, echo off the guns.

The cop leans toward me again. The cruiser stops. "He was shot bad" he says quietly, nodding gently. I feel the soft in his eyes. "Actually, bad ain't the word man." He looks at me, I look at him, ten seconds is a minute. "Two shots from a sawed-off shotgun, one in the back, one in the chest." He shakes his head, turns his focus to the street, checks me again with a couple of quick glances. I stare ahead as the world cruises by in silent washes of falling tears.

FOURTEEN

I lie on my side in bed, arm beneath me numb, aching, throbbing. I don't bother to move, don't bother to pull my arm from its deadened position. I wait for five o'clock. I have been waiting for five o'clock for four hours. I wait for the local news, the familiar faces of newscasters on the live soundless TV.

KRON 4 Evening News glares the screen. A camera man stands his position next to the mechanical silhouette of his camera, straddles electric cords running across the floor. The All American weatherman mouths through white pages of notes. The sports reporter smiles his round red face, chats up giggling female anchors.

The camera zooms on Wendy Tokuda, black hair cut pixie style, gray suit coat, white collared blouse beneath. Her face jumps in playful expressions.

"Hail in San Jose? Tornadoes in the Central Valley? What on earth is going on?" She turns to Pam Moore, the second anchor shaking her smiling head. The camera pans them both, zooms to Pam, lines cut across her brow as she looks straight into the camera.

"Plus. Whose finger was in the bowl of Wendy's chili? After nearly three months, this question still eludes the authorities, leaving many to wonder why no one has yet to come forward. These stories and more after this commercial break."

"What about Maynard?" I shout at the TV "What the fuck about Maynard?" I grab the remote, mute a commercial for erectile dysfunction. Fucking media! "What about Maynard?" I mumble turning into the pillow, burying my face, breathing in the smell of detergent.

The news reports are all the same on channels 2, 4, 5 and 7, at 5, 6, 9 and 11 o'clock. The shooting buried deep in the newscast, just before the weather, just after steroid use in major league baseball. Barry Bonds tiredly claims his innocence. Aakil, Reginald, the homeless man celebrated as heroes for tackling a disgruntled ex-staff member and stripping him of his sawed-off shotgun. The police report there was an axe, a pistol and a shotgun laid out on the front counter with enough ammunition to take us all out. "It appears he intended to 'go postal', to take each staff member out as they walked through the door" states a detective investigating the scene. "If it wasn't for the courage of these three men . . ." His thumb points over his shoulder to the curb where Aakil, Reginald, and Vincent sat this morning. The homeless man now has a name.

But what of the rest of it? What about the stalking? Does anyone care we were terrorized for a fucking week? Does anyone care we asked for help repeatedly and received nothing, not even fucking reassurances? Anger assails me through the night. I cannot sleep. I cannot close my eyes. I imagine myself interviewed over and over and over again. I tell my story to a packed room of reporters. I tell my fears to a packed audience who cares. I ask for help and they reply with how can they help. I stare at the ceiling. I cannot sleep.

FIFTEEN

He is there as he is most every day, playing the violin at the base of the escalator lifting me from the bright lights and white marble floors of the Civic Center Station, violin case lined in red felt open like a hungry mouth to feed. Only a few scattered coins lie at the bottom among wrinkled sheets of lined white paper scribbled with his music. If he is there when I pass I dig deep in my pockets for a dollar, coins to toss onto the stacks of music he has written. I wish I could see them for myself, wish I had the balls to ask. Not that I read music, just want to see what he believes.

His stance that of a warrior, wide spread legs, bent knees push left with the thrust of his bow, pull right in slow sorrowful retreat. He surges then jerks back, falling into his reckless abandon playing. The yellow hair of his bow falls frayed strands, in pain through each pull, a screaming across un-tuned strings pulled tight enough to simply make a sound. Screech, eyes widen into his brow, groan, narrow into the tip of his nose. His mouth opens high, stretches his enthusiasm toothless gum to toothless gum, pursing sharp and pointed, tongue wetting lips in a passionate sweep.

    He must be in his sixties. Street life bags his eyes, cheek crevices make way for laughter, smiles for passerby. Dreadlocks fall under a worn black beanie, knitted yarn a lint ball mix, thin strands stretching. He tucks his gray plaid sports coat into blue plaid pants, wraps a belt around his waist, never bothering with the belt loops.

    In front of him a metal music stand, bent and leaning into its own defined balance. A wrinkled sheet of paper, folded creases stands proudly under the gaze of intense eyes. What is it he sees? What is it he believes?

    I pull a worn dollar bill from my wallet, feel it roll in my tightening hand. I say two prayers into that dollar bill before I drop it carefully into his stacks of sheet music. The first is that he find enlightenment and liberation through his unwavering devotion, his unconditional giving and perseverance through suffering. The second is for myself, that I might capture just one glimpse of his unquestionable faith.

SIXTEEN

I thought I saw Maynard again today walking down a gray empty Tenderloin street. A leap of my heart caused the wind in me to blow cold and sharp as I stood on the stretch of sidewalk in my worn suede boots. Heart pounding. Skin flushing. Hands trembling. Eyes fixed. There he came, owning the street in his masculine strides, one shoulder thrown before the other, pumping his arm, his momentum hard and driven. He wore that heavy gold denim Carhartt jacket, the kind plumbers wear, and ironworkers and cattlemen; it boxed a stiff square image as his head peeked out with curious eyes like a tortoise from its shell. He seemed so protected in that jacket, almost invincible from the maddening world, the world we debated about, the world we lusted after, the world we tried to ignore when it got to be too much. Too many times I wanted to reach my hand under the thick of his shell, feel warm soft skin, the beating of his heart. I thought I saw him again today, but he's been dead now for some time.

I am obsessed with death these days. Since that day in May, just over a year and a half ago with the gunshots still firing in my mind, the lure of death is a warm dull soft light behind my closed eyes bidding me to lay down my weariness in comfort and ease. Daily the silent mantras run my mind like water dripping tediously from a faucet, just kill me, it should have been me, just kill me, it should have been me. I daze the question into my gnawed cuticle as I examine the recesses of my fingernails for another corner of skin to tear and bleed. Which is worse, bleeding to death from sawed-off shotgun wounds or living day in and day out in this fucking red pool of guilt?

In the dark of my apartment I wait for Darnell, sunk in my oversized red chair. I've had a couple beers. I belch. The release is good. My belly relaxes, feels less bloated. He is an hour late. Easy to be angry. Easy to forgive. 45 minutes early yesterday, an hour late today. Time is a dart game to a man who wears no watch, does not own a phone. I think of Darnell walking through the door like he does. Sometimes he owns the place, throwing his jacket and hoodie on the couch, stretching out, kicking off his shoes. Sometimes he owns the world, piling plastic bags of produce on the kitchen table, throwing his hands back and wide at his sides, proud of his forage at the food bank, pride of the hunter with his kill. Sometimes he owns me, stepping right up to me and gathering me away from my writing, pulling me towards the big of the bed, pulling clothes off in a shuffle with one thing on his mind. And then sometimes he slips through the front door as quiet as light rising at dawn, brushing his cheek against mine, lips soft kissing me away as he fades into the shadows of the room. I wish he was slipping in right now to end this waiting.

However Darnell comes he never weathers blue. I never see him sad; perhaps he pockets depression at the door before he rings. If I were in his shoes living in the street the way he does I'd be dead. Depressed or dead; either by my own hand or someone else's. "I think about suicide often" I told him the other day when he asked how low was my low.

"Suicide angers God." He did not look at me

"How do you know?"

"Because my granddaddy was a preacher and he told me so." He casts his eyes sharply across the room as if recalling a long ago Sunday school lesson. "God don't want his children killin' themselves. He put us here to experience life, to learn, to love, and most of all to not cause harm. That includes our own selves." He sizes me up with the corner of his eye. "I don't know how comfortable I feel dating someone who is suicidal." My eyes stab at the word dating. I was not aware he considered himself dating me, me dating him.

"I don't have the balls to kill myself." But I couldn't hold the challenge of his stare. My swallow hits the empty of my stomach; it was the first time I found myself afraid of losing him, dating or not. Don't leave me, I nearly panicked aloud, please don't leave me. My arms feel empty. He ain't mine, never was mine, never will be mine. Stronger urges gather him; I know this to be true when his eyes go wandering, when his curiosity is captured by the silence he stares into.

    Suicide. Darnell was the second person I ever was able to say the word aloud to. Of all the people I knew through my years I thought he would understand

    "Haven't you ever thought about it?"
    "What's that?"
    "Killing yourself?"
    "Only once, but I did the right thing,"
    "What was that?"
    "5150'd myself and prayed my way through." I thought about it for a minute, thought about Dennis Dickey, a former client of mine, sitting on the thin mattress of a metal bed, seventh floor, San Francisco General Hospital Psyche unit. He tried to kill himself, can't recall how though. I thought of my friend Amber and wondered if she had ever 5150'd herself.

    "My friend Amber killed herself." I continued.
    "She's gonna burn in hell." If I believed in heaven the conviction of his words would matter, instead I let his faith settle like dust between us.

    "She spent years convincing my friend Sylvia and me that a flawed cosmic intervention landed her here on planet earth. She was never supposed to take human form." Darnell pulls away eyeing me like I'm a crazy motherfucker. "She thought she was extra-terrestrial." His distance heightens with a lift of his brows. "Really, she did." I flip my mind back to the story Sylvia told me seven years ago, the day after they found Amber's body. "One day she pitched her tent in a soft green meadow in Oregon, swallowed a bottle of sleeping pills, drank half a quart of Jack Daniels, tied a plastic bag around her neck with rubber bands and went to sleep." The image of her body laying there for days in the heat of summer with flies buzzing around her tent welled me with tears. Darnell just stared at my matter of fact like it was shit on the dining room table.

"I wish I had your courage Amber" I say aloud but then shake my head down to a slow chuckle sway. "But there are no soft green meadows in the Tenderloin and I sure as hell can't stand the taste of Jack Daniels." A smile sweeps me up, lifts my posture in the chair, pulls me to standing. Tears rain inside, my breath runs short. I head for the tea pot, time for a Klonopin. I keep my Klonopin hidden there in the tea pot. Benzos to cut the edge. Three scrips, three docs, three ways to kill myself the more refills I stash.

"Who was she?" Darnell asked hours later after I had nearly forgotten the conversation.

"Who was who?"

"That lady that gone off and killed herself?"

"She was a friend of Sylvia's and mine. Sylvia who I talk to on the phone."

Darnell nodded familiar, "For hours on end" he mumbled recalling a conversation I had with Sylvia the other night. All of thirty minutes, maybe forty-five, alright maybe an hour.

"Amber introduced Sylvia and me twenty years

ago. We were living out in the woods at a retreat center in the mountains of Oregon." I lean into him, his full mouthed hunger convincing me he had been wanting the same, that is, end the fucking conversation and get on with getting naked. We fuck, but I can't tease Amber out of my mind.

SEVENTEEN

He wore a blue suit. How handsome I thought, how perfect he looked despite appearing as if he had put on a little weight, especially in his face, brown skin splotched in shades of lighter lifts, shades of darker hollows. His chest stretched strong and wide beneath his lapels, his white rose boutonniere was pinned with a pearl-headed straight pin just over his heart. "My, my, my." I said aloud hoping the words would quit the tremble of my hands, give strength to my weakening knees. But the words took me into a deeper stare of him. I had been so used to seeing him in his Carhartt jacket. His man was his tight blue jeans, the weight of his heavy round basket of a crotch, Big Dog t-shirt, nipples pushing through, musk trailing his exaggerated gestures or quick dashes about the office, always jumping somewhere. I teared up taking him in a little deeper. That is what I remembered about Maynard most. Moving always moving. I used to wonder what was coursing through those veins of his to make him jump the way he did; feet always tapping, knees always bouncing, hands always shuffling papers in hopes of creating order out of a chaotic desk of disability applications, client files, chewed pencils and candy wrappers. But nothing coursed those veins as my eyes waited for him to smile or call me an asshole in jest as he used to. I wanted to pull away; instead I wondered what it would have been like to have kissed him, just fucking kissed him once. "Se-xy moth-er fuck-er." My clenched teeth holding back the tears allowed the words but I didn't feel the heart of my voice. My fingertips reached out and traced the curves of his jaw line, neck, and shoulder, picked a blonde curl of mine off the smooth navy suit. I managed a smile recalling the view from my desk to his, of how day in and day out I found myself stopping my stare of him to gaze at the stretch of carpet between us to the papers stacking my desk, to the traffic surging outside the converted storefront office windows. And there he lay beneath my tearing eyes, new blue suit, coffin framing the death of him. The shock recalling Maynard's funeral leaves me lost in the quiet of my breath. So long ago it seems. Perhaps it seems that way because each goddamn day is a tortoise. Heavy. Dull. Slow.

    The yellow school bus in the street below my studio window tells me it is seven-ten in the morning. I may not know if it is Monday or Tuesday or even fucking Friday because the dumb I fall into these days leaves me with a goddamn careless attitude. Don't give a shit about the day, the time, the month or even the fucking season for that matter, but I do know those hollering school kids are lined up with their oversized Scooby-Doo backpacks, parents looking on as they board, hands waving goodbye, every fucking week day morning at seven-ten. The line moves slowly. The fear they must go through, those kids, those parents, the stretch of separation between the corner bus stop and wherever the school bus takes them. A man stands with his three children, a baby in the stroller. His blue pants and shirt are covered in dashes of different colored paints, he wears a baseball cap. Hard working family man I think to myself, so seldom do I see the likes of him in these streets. Darnell says it's because I don't look hard enough. The man holds both his children's hands in one of his until they reach the school bus door; his other hand secures the stroller. Hugging him goodbye they are lost in the size of him. I close my eyes and imagine the strong, calloused skin of Maynard's hands, his boy taking his daddy's hand on his way to school just like those kids. Whose hand does the boy hold now? Whose arm does he curl under while sitting on the couch watching a movie on TV? Whose hand packs his lunch into his Scooby- Doo backpack, pats his ass on the way out the door?

 The pastels of the funeral home leave me nauseous and bored sitting on a blue Naugahyde couch with nowhere to escape to but the knot of my hands in my lap; stiff furniture, paintings of the sea, heavy gold frames, fake plants reflecting the brave white lights too loudly. I sit by the office in hopes no one will bother crossing the long room to speak to me; not knowing who I am perhaps they will think I am there on other business, perhaps they might think I worked in the funeral home but then again they probably saw me stumbling up the pews to where Maynard is laid out, returning fifteen minutes later bleary-eyed and stupefied.

    Sitting on the couch my eyes lift up and down the wallpaper, vertical lines of vines, never see wall paper anymore, at least not this ugly. Brass candelabras with dusty white candles never burnt; white turning gray from the exhaust of Market Street. I have been on this fucking couch for God knows how long after seeing Maynard knotting my hands, can't manage to say hello to anyone. Me, alone in the chapel staring into that silver pillowed coffin while the others, whoever they are, I assume family, hover in the lobby. Nobody looks my way, I can hardly look theirs. Yet in the middle of a circle of six nodding heads with soft spoken lips, Maynard's nine-year-old boy Keith stands in his new blue suit, chin lifting to be seen, neck stretching to be equal among the adults surrounding him, big ears reaching to not miss a single word. I search the boy's face to see his father in him because that's what you're supposed to say at funerals; oh you look so much like him, that's what you say. Your daddy must have been so proud of you. Is that what you say? You're the man of the house now. Stay strong, be proud. OH FUCK! What the fuck do you say? What the FUCK do you say? Sorry your daddy took the bullets meant for my tired old white ass? Sorry your daddy and I argued about calling the police the week before when the fucker Grayson was stalking me?

"Call the cops!" My staff pleaded.

"Oh the fucking cops won't do anything," whined my boss who sat comfortably a few blocks away in a secured building.

"The cops will only make him more angry than he is!" Maynard insisted with the palm of his hand slapping his bouncing knee to drive the point home.

"Call the cops!" The staff pleaded.

"I know the man's anger! We all seen that nigga's temper!" Maynard shouted his words high and hard over the rest of ours. Maynard stood, his chair rolled back when he did. "You call the cops and that fucker is liable to rush these fucking doors!" The fear silenced us all. Maynard's insistence won.

My eyes return to the circle in the parlor of the funeral home. Keith picks his nose with a quick jab of his index finger; an adult hand is there to pull his small finger away. The boy's mouth and nose wrinkle and stretch, distorting the soft brown round of his face; trying to scratch the depth of the nostril he lifted the back of his hand to the side of his nose. The adult hand is there as swift as before, this time pointing him across the lobby of the funeral home, past the tapping of my foot to the men's bathroom. A reprieve I think to myself, the boy could be in there for a while blowing his nose, picking his nose, lost in the bathroom stall. I won't have to hear the sweet of his voice, his eyes of curiosity staring into me when I take his hand to introduce myself. As he passes my back pushes deep into the Naugahyde, nausea greens my face, my eyes focus on the wrinkles of my barely ironed white shirt.

Lost in my folded hands I recall Maynard talking about his mother the first day I took my new position as Associate Director; we were getting to know each other, him explaining to me, "Sometimes I get here a little early because I gotta get my boy Keith to school like at eight. So I get here eight-thirty, make a pot of coffee, read the paper, check the messages on the phone machine, maybe go to the Post Office to get the mail."

"How old is your boy?" I asked that first morning.

"Nine, third grade. Same elementary school I went to."

"No shit."

"He's even got one teacher that I had when I was in school."

"Damn she must be old."

Maynard laughed a "Fuck You" at me. Then his eyes went looking kind of far away. "My mama was so proud . . ." His eyes returned looking hard right into me. "Our family, seven kids in all, raised in Hunter's Point was the only family on the block where one of us kids wasn't killed." I looked at him with a puzzled expression, not really getting it. He understood I needed a bit more. "All our neighbors had lost a kid to gunfire at one time or another. In high school we went to funerals more than we went to church." I don't think my eyes blinked in his matter of fact.

EIGHTEEN

    Depression is a clock which moves backwards, forwards and not at all. Depression is the shit I think about that doesn't mean shit, doesn't solve shit but just spins the second hand of my brain round and round. I should pay rent. Did I deposit the check? Will it clear in time? I need to buy beer. Do I have cash? Can I write a check? I should check my balance. What if there is not enough to pay rent? I should go to the bank. What's for breakfast? Is it time for a beer? And on it goes.
    It is these thoughts I drill into the white landscape on the wall by my bed; a lighter shade of gray that foggy morning, a brighter version of the same, the slow tumble of the afternoon hours becoming as black as city lights will allow at midnight and thereafter; not really black but wanting to be blue. Hours pass,

a day, maybe two. I close my eyes. Depression is like that at times, wanting to be something other than it is, wanting to be dead, wanting to be loved, wanting to be happy and normal. It wants to be like before, before depression, but what was it like before? I can't recall. My therapist sent me home with the task of listing ten things that make me happy. Winning was the only thing I could come up with. Winning what, he asked. Winning fucking anything I replied; a scrabble game, an argument, being the first in line. I almost cried when I lost three straight games of solitaire the other day. Funny how in my mind it usually implies misery for others in their loss; perhaps I seek an even playing field. Depression wants to be somewhere else, with someone else, some other time and so the clock moves, or doesn't move at all. Indecision beds me here. Shit, the shit I think is just the shit I think and the second hand spins.

    Depression is the phone waiting to ring, staring at me, asking me who I can call. The answer is no one because no one understands. Depression is the phone ringing but too ashamed to pick it up. It's the phone ringing again, Darnell calling, the front door speaker phone, the roar of buses in the back ground, the honking of horns, the voice asking or is it pleading, "Can I come up?" I buzz him in and count the six flights it takes to come to my door. I know this because both elevators were out all last week. I climbed those stairs punching anger into every step for having to climb. It took five days before they got around to fixing them. I did not leave my apartment until they were fixed. I buzz him in all the while knowing he will be much quicker taking the elevator, pushing the accordion gate, the slam of it closing behind him announcing his arrival, me able to hear all this way down the hall even though I am buried in my pillows. I wish I had let the call go to voicemail. Why did I let him in?

    Depression is my crumpled heap on the bed, hiding myself in my thoughts, in my anger, in the scattering of pillows, the roll of the unused comforter, the blanket in heavy curbs. I do not move when the yellow light of the door opens and falls across the bed like daylight filling a church, his mumbling the deep chanting of monks but there sure isn't anything holy about this. I wish I hadn't let him in. The door closes. The mumbling pauses. His footsteps are silent, or is he standing there not knowing what to do. My predictable smiling of his arrival, the hunger of my ass, the pounding of my heart lie like corpses in the room. Black is blue, blue is black, depression is both and in he slips, his words quieting with the fall of each of his steps to my lack of response.

    " . . . Understanding E equals m c squared suggests consciousness exists . . ." I feel him watching me. ". . . after death simply because the perpetuation of energy . . ." He leans to look at me more closely; his hand runs the length of my body beneath the blanket. ". . . of creating one's own reality is dependent on . . . motion . . . You all right?"

    Silence. How do I ask him to leave? He is soft around the foot of the bed; the balls of his tiptoeing feet lead his eyes in examination of me lying here in shame. Him seeing me this way, I sink further beneath the pillows. He pauses unsure of his trespass. His jacket peals away from his shoulders. His boots are heeled off one at a time. His belt buckle clanks in its undoing, falls a thud to the floor, his shirt, socks and underwear tumble in a hush. I cry.

    The wind of Darnell is the lift of the sheets and blanket, cool air, his knowing, his breath, his sensitivity, him sliding behind me. His body is warm. He spoons into me. I feel his chest my back, his thighs my thighs, his hand palming my head softly, his lips kissing my shoulder like the white of me is porcelain. His voice lifts, reaching, lullabys me, "Sometimes you can't listen to those voices baby cause they git you all fucked up in the head . . ." He kisses me. He strokes my head gently.

NINETEEN

I pause before I knock on the bathroom door. Splashing and Darnell's words mix with the rush of water filling the tub. It's a familiar sound lately, a familiar routine, much like the scouring scratch of Ajax as I scrub the dark rings in the tub when he is done, like the sigh of me picking the towel up off the floor and hanging it over the shower curtain rail, routine like screwing the cap back on the toothpaste and rinsing the sink where clumps of paste fell, like replacing a new head on the razor and calling him back into the bathroom to shave the spots on the back of his head he missed. All that will come soon enough. Right now I don't want to interrupt his time in the bathroom. I imagine it is the only time in his life he gets to be alone; no privacy in the shelter, the soup lines, the Career Center, the subway. He's hit the streets all day looking for a job. I push my way through my resistance. "Hey Darnell." I knock and open the door. "I'm ordering Chinese, what you got a taste for?" His suit is in a pile on the bathroom floor. "Hey, ya want me to hang this up?"

"Shrimp fried rice." I smile, could have guessed. I pick up his pants, his shirt, his tie, his coat with quick sweeps intending to back out the door without chilling the warmed room. Red prints on the white tiles at the edge of the tub stop me. Deep red and smeared, an oversized fingerprint.

"What's that?" I point.

"Nothin'. Just bleeding from the pores of my feet." He lies reclined in the tub, one foot crossing his knee; he picks at skin surrounding what seem like blisters on his big toe, the ball of his foot.

"You alright?"

He picks. "Yea, just been walkin' too much." Wrinkles his nose in pain, eyebrows focusing hard and pointed, picks dead skin some more.

TWENTY

Christmas trees or human beings, not sure which is which. They lay along the wet Leavenworth sidewalk in the late afternoon drizzle, end to end for just part of a block or so. Discarded, yet having once been celebrated they wait, wrapped in plastic, old bed sheets or under the moistened shine of wet green-blue-black Hefty garbage bags, waiting with one last hope for the sun to break through and warm their bones or for the garbage trucks to haul their bristled branches away. Christmas trees or human beings? My eyes wander from the rounded breadth of imagined wide branches or shoulders down the coning and narrowing length of them to discover the tip of tinsel strewn tree tops or leather worn pairs of untied boots. My shuddering mixes sorrow, helplessness, a nagging vulnerability coupled with the quickening of the dropping temperature. I hear my father interrupt my thoughts, 'the coldest parts of the day are sunrise and sunset,' an hour or so away as my hands dig deep in my jacket pockets for more secure warmth. My shoulders rise to prevent the chill I witness on the street from falling over my collar and racing down my spine.

TWENTY-ONE

    I lean into the mirror, push the tip of my nose up with my pinky to expose the forest of nose hairs growing thick and unmanageable within. If left alone I am sure these hairs would point themselves out my nostrils. Wouldn't that be fucking attractive? Thick wiry hair, so thick it could be twined and used for rope. For many years I have struggled with my eyes focusing on the tips of the tweezers, inserting, locating and hoping I have at last secured a hair between the narrow tips. Well practiced, I clamp, breathe deep and pull with an exhale cringing in pain as the sting flashes in streaks up my nose. Tears hit my eyes. I wipe them away to see clearly and insert the tweezers again.
    Hair seems to ritually mark transitions in my life, the soft fluff of puberty cupping a non-stop erection ushered masturbating into my dirty tube socks in

the middle of the night. I would fantasize shadows of gathering men standing at my bedside, slipping in between the sheets with me, much like my brother used to except they would not leave me bleeding. Just hoping for a fucking better outcome I guess. Shadows of faceless men with strong calloused hands, one after another, coming to me because they wanted to be with me, really be with me. Fantasies became reality when I came home from college; the flame of red razor burn swelled the circle of my mouth and the stretch of my neck after kissing an unshaven man for hours on end. I tried to eat that beard of his, lips gnawing the strength of his jaw line causing my lips to fatten in raw sensitivity. Without warning I was sent scrambling for a lie. "Danny what's going on with your face?" My father asked the next morning at breakfast. I dropped into my Cheerios.

"Uh. I don't know, uh, I think I am allergic to that new brand of pimple medication I picked up at K-Mart. Uh, I think . . ." I never thought he noticed such things.

In my thirties my hair grew long, a free spirit I thought I was. I followed robed gurus and read big books promising my feet would touch this world more gently. My hair fell in golden waves and locks over my shoulders. In the winter I grew a beard and on a cold January night I was picked up by a man who took me to the Civic Center Hotel, a smack hotel on Market Street, heroin flowed down the hallways like a flood. On a skinny wiry bed he insisted I fuck him. "I never have" I mumbled trying not to interrupt the race of passion.

"Never have what?" He pulled on my screaming dick.

"Never fucked a man before." He positioned the head of my dick right up against his ass, pulled his hand away, spit three times into it, lubed up my dick with his spit and pulled me into him.

"Well ya can't say that no more baby." He pushed into me as I slid deep into him. The astonishment of being inside of someone caused fear to stretch my dick harder and further, almost pushing it outside of itself. Deeper I went. It was hot in there. It was really hot. And soft. And supple. And wet. I swore I felt the pulse of him. And as I pounded his ass that wiry old bed yelled. Yelled and jumped away from the wall, skating across the floor. I could hear shouting in the next room, the other side of the thinning walls, shouting, telling us to keep it down. "KEEP IT DOWN!" But that didn't stop me cause I kept thinking I was gonna come.

"I'M GONNA COME! I'M GONNA COME!" I kept pounding the shit out of his ass as he clung to the bars of the headboard above him. The old bed continued to bounce; the shouting next door gave into amplified heavy metal rock. My hair flew. My long blonde sweat dampened hair trampolined from my back, my shoulders and my chest into the air. I lifted his legs, spread them wide to the sides as the skinny of me screamed into a rib filled stretch.

"FUCK ME JESUS! FUCK ME!" His ass opened deeper for me and deeper I went and went and went. "FUCK ME JESUS! FUCK ME!" My eyes opened to the bulging rage of the whites of his eyes against his brown skin burning red. Eyes raging into me. He believed! He believed! He believed Jesus was fucking him! The bed was now in the middle of the room. My pounding lost the hit of intense desire as my eyes saw the reflection of me in the vanity mirror. Hair strewn across my face, caught in my beard. My back curved, arms wide, nailed into the air by the soles of his feet, heart pounding so fierce it was popping through my ribs. Jesus spread on the cross I was. He came screaming his name. "JEEEESUUUS!" I withdrew. Hit with the stench of feces, I toweled myself off and swore I would never fuck a man again.

So now it is nose hairs need clipping, eyebrows need plucking and the occasional wild hair sprouting in my ear calling for a good yank if I can pinch it between my fingernails. Hair grows where it shouldn't, on one shoulder but not the other, between the knuckles of my fingers, in random patches on my back. Hair, once curling blonde and admired now glows white and gray and is shunned. They say if you are gay and gray, ya might as well be ninety. I gaze into the mirror, follow the endless lines of age, shy from the sad I see in the swim of my blue eyes, try to stop the trembling tweezers in my hand. I hate mirrors. The only thing they are good for is to watch myself getting fucked.

TWENTY-TWO

Down aisle 4-B in Walgreens I glide, the blur of Hallmark pink and red either side nags the question, 'Who is your Valentine?' Darnell? I doubt it, can't expect scheduled celebrated romance from a man who lately can't remember what day of the week it is. Who the fuck needs a card or flowers or candy anyway? He demonstrated his love the other day when he showed up after being missing for three weeks. "I'll make ya breakfast." I shuddered to think what the kitchen would look like in the end.

"Ya want some help?"

"No. I'm gonna cook a man's breakfast, none of this 1980's boutique breakfasts you serve."

"What's a boutique breakfast?"

"You know, perfect this perfect that in small portions around the plate. Ya leave a man hungry. Waste my ass away eatin' 1980's boutique . . ." he trailed into the kitchen to cook a man's breakfast talking to himself all the way through. Always thought I made plenty. Eight scrambled eggs, four nuked potatoes cut and browned in a skillet and a whole package of Jimmy Dean Sausage later I sat in front of a plate heaping with food. I realized he needed to be eating more than what I had been serving him, just his way of letting me know that I suppose. Regardless, I'd rather have him cook on random occasions like that than bring me flowers on a celebrated day.

"Will you be my Valentine?" A motion activated dancing teddy bear sings a nasal song while sitting on the cash register at the pharmacy counter in the far back reaches of Walgreens. It holds a big red heart in its claws while it shakes its butt. I want to backhand it into the cold and flu section, slap it into the rows of Nyquil. Stupid sentimental shit ain't gonna cheer my ass up. The fact is that even in clean, semi-sterile and well lit stores like this, the pharmacy always reeks grim, diseased, and infectious. Stupid dancing bear doesn't change that.

Six out of my seven meds are ready. Gotta wait. Call the Doc. Fax the pharmacy.   Bill the insurance. Fill the scrip. Hand me my shopping bag full of tenuous life support and I will be on my merry way. This twenty year old routine of HIV meds is fucking old. I think sometimes it would be so easy to stop. To just stop the meds and the doctor visits and the blood draws and the refills and the trips back to Walgreens where I sit in a line of blue square chairs next to death wheezing, pain moaning, phlegm coughing, snot sneezing people until they call my name and jump I go. It would be so easy to usher in that slow death, that seductive lazy decline of a failing body without that shopping bag of support, a spiral down the long dark barrel of a shotgun. Why didn't I die in the eighties when the rest of my world did?

    Who is my Valentine anyway? If asked I couldn't say, wouldn't say, too ashamed to say. I hear it now. "Darnell who? Oh the man I have been sleeping with for 3 months now, minus three weeks that is, because he went missing you see. Missing, yea missing, as in possibly arrested for shoplifting, possibly hospitalized because Liza Minnelli, Robert Downey Junior and a host of others were screaming in his head telling him to go on and reach over and lift that fifth of Smirnoff Vodka from the well when the bartender wasn't looking, or possibly he went tweaking with Tina and a party of muscle boy gang bangers." You never know with Darnell, he didn't offer to explain when I asked him "Where ya been?"

    As if in a race against time Darnell's jaw rolled. "Did you know that Robert Downey Junior lived in the Castro? He should have never been busted for drugs. His father is just like him. Just like Liza Minnelli telling me to pick that money up off the night stand at the Becks Hotel. It turned black in my hands. What money? What fucking money? Then they accuse Liza of ripping them off. But she don't do drugs no more, at least not like Robert Downey Junior does. She's training to be an analyst. Astral projection. Nudging me, nudging me. Yes means no, no means yes! I hate that fucking shit! They called the cops! The make-up police. I had to run!" I walk away.

No. No Valentine. No. I could never see taking him home for the holidays either. My father would glare at me like I had brought shame to the family yet again, like when my brother outed me back in eighty-one and left my father not knowing how to explain it to the relatives. Or when I tested positive, never knew the man to be more silent. Or back in eighty-six when I dated three men at one time. Antonio, Antonio, and Tony. It was hard to keep track. "Fucking whore!" my father slammed in the lounge of Outback Steak House when I told him I was dating three men at the same time because I couldn't decide on who I wanted the most. "My son is a fucking whore!" He took his scotch and water and stood in the lobby until our table was ready. So I can just see my father's response to Darnell. He would glare at me when Darnell pulls his Liza Minnelli, glare and say nothing. Then he'd go sit in the other room. No. I can't tell anyone. No one has the capacity to understand, to look beyond word salad and see the brilliance of a mind, the longing of a heart, the loneliness of a soul yearning to love, spoon, and cook a man's breakfast undisturbed.

Just leave me the fuck alone! All ya'll! I scream my own Liza in my head, sitting in the blue square chair as judgment comes marching through a myriad of voices; my father, my family, my relatives, my friends, my neighbors. My fingernails pick and scratch and pull at a cuticle on my thumb. I lift the cuticle to my mouth and gnaw in quick little bites, wanting to catch hold and tear the flesh away. The shout of judgment comes screaming again. Yea call me crazy! Yea call me wasting my fucking time when I am capable of, and deserving of, a better man than the man I call my own! Yea call me an addict when men slip in when Darnell is in his suit, out looking for a job! Yea call me an addict when in the morning I search Craigslist to see if any man in the neighborhood is in need of an early blow and go! Yea call me a sex addict when I lie in my bed sex sore and red rubbed raw still insisting on more! All ya'all can just fuck yourselves!

In aisle 1-A you'll find makeup and hair color to turn you into someone you're not, 5-A you'll find your fucking Good and Plenty, Snickers, Hershey's and Milky Way bars! 7-A your fucking Doritos and Cheetos and Pringle potato chips! 7-B People Magazine and the all the fucking idle gossip you crave cause ya ain't got no life of your own! And while you are there pick up the latest Danielle Steele or Stephen King! In aisle 8 you'll find your fucking Coca Cola so when you take your fat ass home and sit in your fucking recliner with your remote control in your sugar trembling hands you'll have enough fuel to channel surf your cable TV! Leave-me-the-fuck-alone! I rip the cuticle, blood runs. I suck my thumb.

"Mr. Hill." I step to the counter to get my prescriptions.

"Will you be my Valentine?" The bear shakes its ass.

TWENTY-THREE

I recall being a boy looking forward each month to National Geographic magazine coming in the mail. I would count thirty days between the deliveries and race down the long drive to the mail box day after day until it came, and would wash my hands before slipping the brown paper sleeve away just like my mom would tell me. I don't remember the year, perhaps mid to late sixties, but I do recall the rush of excitement as I stared into the green, the towering green majesty of Machu Pichu in Peru. Getting there became my dream over the years as the photographic pages wore thin from constant flipping and eventually were tossed into the recycling bin. So on my thirtieth birthday, six months after the positive test results with the whisper of death shouldering me, I hitchhiked my way through the Andes, through the Inca Valley and before dawn climbed God knows how many hundreds of feet to the ancient temple city. I stood at the end of a path, high, twelve thousand feet high, standing in a cloud, seeing nothing but cloud, feeling nothing but the chilling movement of wet and white against my skin, waiting for the lift of the cloud to reveal the path again so I could continue on my quest. The clouds cleared, the white lifted and the dream became real revealing the deepest awe of my heart, open and breathing, the ancient city of the Incas spreading wide below me. I stumbled a few steps disbelieving I had made it. Everything became possible in that moment. I stretched my arms into victory and felt the potential of so many dreams, not just my own. In one breath the city hid in the clouds, in another it was revealed in the gray of dawn. The world fell away thousands of feet below these spindly mountain tops, not even an echo could reach me. I turned to my sides, both left and right, waited for the newly gathered clouds to rise and reveal but there was no one to share this lifelong awaited moment with. All I felt was the well of alone, deeper than that mountain high.

 I dream of eating Chicago deep dish pizza with three feet of hard frozen snow on the ground, barbeque in Memphis with a cold beer in the heavy humidity of a hot summer's day while listening to some wannabe blues band, or to eat bottomless bowls of gumbo in New Orleans, corn bread on the side, deep fried soft shell crab on the way and all you smell in the air is burnt grease and spilled beer. But what is it worth if there is no one there to say it needs salt, to tell me I've had enough to drink, to argue which restaurant to eat in or to pause in the rush of Chicago, Memphis, New Orleans or any other fucking city in the world, look into my eyes, and agree without words that this sure ain't home, nor would we ever want it to be. My dreams are a bit more tempered these days, lacking the balls of challenge and adventure they once knew. I am surprised I dream at all. For a number of years after Peru, I only held the thought of next week and my next meal in my mind as I waited and waited and waited to die. The courage to dream was as ethereal as the dream itself. Twenty years and still not dead, so what the fuck, might as well dream a little. Dream that Darnell will find work and get housed. Dream that I might write some published work someday. Dream of being able to afford a movie, a play or a Broadway show. Dream that I might wake up one morning and find my body with developed biceps and triceps and pecs and abs and quads rather than looking like a fucking marshmallow with tooth picks stuck in the sides. Yet every time I go fucking dreaming, the wander of my heart finds the lonely in its end. So much for fucking dreams.

    I am drunk. Drunk on cum. Drunk on lube. Drunk on dick and wine. I am dream drunk as nausea takes two steps closer to the bathroom. The world blurs as the doorframe leans and I catch it, lights too bright so I dim them, the stereo slurs a bluesy Duffy love song as I try to make sense of the words.

> *Don't you be wasting all your money*
> *On syrup and honey*
> *Because I'm sweet enough*

Somewhere in the street below shouting slaps through her pause, "Kamala Harris is stalking me just like she is stalking you! I refuse to be part of this citywide reality TV show! They got plasma TV with Lisa Kudrow doing sex acts in a window on the corner of Eddy and Leavenworth! Kamala Harris is watching YOU!"

Don't you be giving every minute
On making a living
Because we've got our love

". . . Investigators forced tests, using me when I told them not to! Costing me a job at Maxwell's! Kamala Harris stalked me and is the cause of uncertainty and will scar you like she scarred me! Plasma TV. . ."

Listen to me
One, two, three
Baby, baby, baby,
Spend your time on me

Nausea passes, my stomach finds footing. Without looking I know it is Darnell. I stand on an edge of tears. I don't dare breathe deep cause I know they will fucking burn my cheeks if I do. I don't dare go to the window because I know he is watching and wondering why I won't let him in. I can hear the innocent sad of his plea, "Baby, why won't you pick up?"

"CAUSE YOU'RE A FUCKING PSYCHO SCREAMING IN THE STREETS!"

The doorframe leans again. I go to catch it but miss. I fall through the empty door, hands giving into banging elbows giving into pounding knees, giving into the cold bathroom tile resting my face. Nausea hits but I can't make it to the fucking toilet. I puke and puke and dry heave and cry.

TWENTY-FOUR

"You look great Daniel!" My psychiatrist's balding hair is wispy thin, standing up on end from the static electricity in his cushy Kaiser office. After directing me to a chair he rubs his large knuckled, skinny fingered hands together like he is trying to warm them up. Maybe friction eases static, but then maybe static is caused by friction. Fuck if I know. He should stop it though because it makes him look like he is the fucking crazy one here. Boring into my chart through his red rimmed glasses he must feel my eyes because he ain't looking at me. He pats his hair down almost self consciously. His bone white fingers drip over the top of his head like glue. He finally smiles my direction as he closes the file and places it on a stack of similar manila file folders on his desk. We must all look the same to him after a while just like all those manila files; empty in the beginning, fold in the center, well tattered by the end, fifty pages of scribbled notes declaring how depressed we are. Different story, same symptoms. So what does he do? Medicate, medicate, medicate. "My, my, I haven't seen you in awhile." Smiling, he grabs the file again and flips it open. "Yea. You cancelled the last appointment six weeks ago . . ." I think back, booty call as I remember though I don't know for certain who it was. Was it Antoine, or Stephan, or Andre? Some French sounding name with a flailing limp wristed queen-ass attitude? Fucked like a rabbit if I recall correctly. "Then I was on vacation for a few weeks before that. And our appointment prior was six weeks before that, my, my, so that means I haven't seen you in just about four months."

"Long time." I watch the slow lift of his hair as he returns the folder to the stack, one skinny ass thread of hair clings to the next and lifts the mess into a web.

"Well you look great!" Endless Kaiser Enthusiasm. "That Remeron, Gabitril combo seems to being doing the trick." That ole college try cheerlead gives me the sickening feeling he thinks we are a fucking team or something. Get out the fucking pom-poms. He smiles at me waiting for a response. Remeron and Gabitril, the third round of antidepressants that left me flat on my emotional ass, left my dick as limp as Larry. Larry is my friend who hasn't had a hard-on for ten years because he is so fucking depressed and taking the meds like it is some sort of religious rite. He told me it didn't matter because he was too old and ugly to fuck anymore anyway. At least the shit gets him up out of bed in the morning, gets his ass moving, gets him to work. That is all that is important to Larry. Now that I think about it, he is too ugly to fuck.

"Is that right Daniel?" I am startled back to his palm patting the top of his head.

"Yes, that's right. I mean no that's not right."

"What is it Daniel?"

"No." I am suddenly uncomfortable because I forgot how I was going to explain.

"Are you telling me the medication isn't working? You look great!"

"I went off my meds." I look out his window towards the bridge I considered jumping just half a year ago. From his office all I can see are the tips of orange peaking above the Presidio trees. The Golden Gate.

"You did what?!"

"I went off my meds." I can still feel the tremble of the bridge under my feet from the rush hour traffic as I headed mid span.

"Why did you do that?"

"PTSD equals put that shit down. Emotionally flat, no fucking dick and the need for Vitamin D." I turn to him; his hair is straight up on end. In fact, now that I think about it, dick is what spun my ass on a dime and got me off that fucking bridge.

"Excuse me? I don't think I understand." His hands white knuckle the arms of his chair.

I glare right into the reflection of light in his glasses. "I need dick." Silence falls hard. I roll my eyes around the room as if looking for someone to help me explain.

Nearly trembling, "I don't understand. You said

you were taking vitamin D?"

"D stands for dick, Doctor." He pales blank. It wasn't dick actually that saved my ass from jumping; his name was Dick, Richard to be exact. Some plain vanilla white dude visiting from the Midwest. And he didn't really save my ass either; he just smiled at me and commented on the breathtaking view.

The psychiatrist rubs his palms together again but with less intensity. "Vitamin D, would you like to say more?" His hair is up.

"I find if I get laid regularly I don't get depressed." His head tilts, his hands are now in prayer position at the end of his nose. "So I call it vitamin D, ya see. If I get fucking dicked enough I am cool. So I came in today to tell ya I don't need to come back 'cause I am cured. No depression, no more meds, no limp dick, I feel great." His fingertips do not separate as his hands pull away from one another, kind of like a spider doing pushups on the mirror.

"I see. Do you have a friend? Uh, I mean a boy friend? I mean, I guess you would call him a lover?"

"No."

Looking at me sideways, "So how do you arrange this? That is, having sex enough to feel good. I mean, forgive me if I am wrong but there must be some regularity to your sexual activities . . ." He smoothes his hair, fingers drip over his head again. I pause and wonder how I am going to answer. I stare out the window and flash back. Standing near the rail of the bridge, listening to Mr. All American, Velveeta Cheese eating, white Midwest Dick was so disbelievingly fucking boring all I could think about was getting some black dick and hearing the sweet scream of orgasm in my ear. Life is dick. Life is feeling alive. Life was more than Midwest Dick had ever experienced in his sorry ass life. After contemplating the jump I figured a good hard dick freaking my ass was all I needed. Shit, just like that, vanilla white Dick took the spring out of my jump, got me off that bridge.

"Oh there's regularity alright."

"Would you like to say more?" Kaiser Enthusiasm has turned Kaiser Inquiry. I mock in my mind, would you like to say more? I wonder if I should tell him it is specifically black dick that lifts my mood.

"I get it regular enough." He continues his wide-eyed gaze, by not saying anything he is demanding more. I feel trapped. "Eight, nine, ten times a week, maybe more, maybe less if it is a bad week."

"A bad week?"

"Yea, ya know, no call from a fuck buddy, no luck on line, no luck in the streets, no time to get over to the bath house. A bad week. Maybe only four, five, six guys."

"Does your therapist know all of this?" The wind is knocked out of me as I think back to Dr. James.

"I don't see my therapist anymore."

"Why is that Daniel?"

"Cause I saw him on Yahoo personals." Trembling words fall from my mouth. "We . . . were a perfect match . . . that is, according to Yahoo." I flash on his smiling pic. "Five out of five hearts! Five out of five!" My eyes search for the peaks of the bridge but the tears burn them closed and I have to wipe them with the heels of my hands. "I told him all that, told him

I read his profile, told him about the match." Taking a deep breath and holding tight because I know I am about to explode . . . "Told him all of that and less than twenty-four fucking hours later he deleted his account from Yahoo!" My body trembles in the tension I hold. I will not fucking cry. I will not fucking break down. I will not look the fool here! Fuck it I already do!

"That upset you." He peers at me with arched eyebrows through the lower half of his lenses.

"Damn fucking right! That fucking pissed me off!" I shudder in my chair, trying to shake off the whole experience but watch the rise of rigidity clamp my shoulders and tighten my belly. My clenching teeth barely allow me to speak. "I mean it's bad enough I spend hours and hours and hours on line trying to get laid only to get rejected ninety-nine times out of a hundred for being too fucking gray, too fucking wrinkled, too fucking out of shape, too fucking HIV-positive!" My chest explodes. "And then to have someone I fucking know, someone I fucking respect, someone who fucking knows every fucking thing about me delete his entire fucking account 'cause he is too ashamed to be seen with me, affiliated with me, let alone considered a fucking perfect five heart match!"

Silence rubs the room raw. "I doubt that is why he deleted his account Daniel. Professionally he has to be careful about . . ."

"Bullshit! He deleted his account 'cause he was too fucking ashamed! Too fucking ashamed!" Through the blur of my tears, the peaks of the Golden Gate rise sharp and pointed over the green of the Presidio trees. "Just two bus rides away." I mumble. Still time to get

there before they close the bridge to pedestrians.
"Let's make another appointment. In the mean time do you have Remeron and Gabitril? My, my, time went by so fast . . ."

TWENTY-FIVE

Pigeons peck and dash along the sidewalk below. Peck and dash. Peck and dash. They fight their way through a torn discarded red and white paper bag from Kentucky Fried Chicken. Pecking at the paper bag, pecking at the cardboard carton inside, pecking at each other as they jump and climb over one another. Peck and dash and climb and jump. Pedestrian feet march by in their threat sending pigeons scattering for safety across the sidewalk, into the gutter, under a parked car. The pigeons return in silent desperation to peck and pull the remains of crusted flesh off an assortment of gnawed chicken bones. A piece of biscuit is pecked into the air. A frenzy of pigeons jump to where it lands. The fluttering of wings against the air is heavy and thick.

Darnell stands on a short raised wall watching

skateboarders rattle and grind along the wide steps leading into one of the concrete government buildings; buildings that stand strong and uncompromising, intimidating even, yet you never see anyone go in or come out except for the grimy Carl's Jr. building on the corner. "I was diagnosed a manipulator." His eyes do not pull from the men-boys skating. He does not think to drop off the wall to stand my equal. I didn't even see him see me coming.

"What kind of diagnosis is that?"

"The kind the psychiatrist gives." His eyes drop to me with a 'that was a stupid fucking question' look. "Ya know, sometimes my head is like a coke machine." He nods in agreement with himself, eyes ripped wide. "People, I mean anyone, come along just as they fucking please, drop a quarter in and take out one of my cokes." He points across the plaza, "They don't take one of his cokes!" Changes directions, "Not hers! And not one of theirs!" His glare blazes into me, finger pointing to the side of his head, "One of my fucking cokes!" This has been Darnell these past few days; loud and intensely delusional.

It was just last week, when he told me he loved me. We must have been snarled legs and arms and sweat for hours, rants of promises, lauds of adulations. Now I think about it, every time we have ever touched we fucked, and every time we fucked we screamed into each other's ears the longing of never being separated. That night he insisted we flip, he inside of me, me inside of him. He wanted to train me to ejaculate "just a lil' bit. Not the whole load baby. Just a lil' bit." He was a master at it. He would come inside me, just a lil' bit, clench his teeth and tremble tight on the edge of his load, face to the ceiling, his chin reaching while the pounding of his heart jilted his body. A deep breath later he would resume his mindful articulate penetration, building slowly passionate again.

It was the first time I was inside of him. The heat of him burning, the depth of him endless. I lay on my back, he straddled me down to the root of me when he stumbled, "I only bottom for guys I love, I mean, guys I like, I mean guys I let . . ."

"Whoa," I pull on the pause between us. "Are you saying you love me?"

His eyes did not meet mine. His attention wavered in the air, nervous. "Now tell me when you're about to come." Still refusing to look at me, he set himself down on the fierce desire of my dick again and again. His face cringed discomfort, mouth opened in a silent moan. His rhythm was slow at first and then became a rage as the sinew of his thighs lifted and dropped him along the length of me, lifted and dropped, grabbing and pulling me with the tensed muscle and tightening ring of his ass.

"I'm coming!"
"Pull back!"
"I'm coming!"
"Pull back!"
"I'm coming!" But hard as I tried, my come screamed into him, bled into him, drained me into him, purging my love for him from me over and again until in the breathlessness of release I moaned defeat, in the arch of adrenaline racing I cringed failure, in the

drop of passion I mouthed I'm sorry. Darnell scooped down into me the hero, arms curling my head, lips kissing me, my heart breaking my chest. He lay for a minute, maybe more, until the pouring heated sweat of us slid him to my side, nuzzled his face into my ear. "I love you" he whispered.

TWENTY-SIX

I am dumbed by the comb-over standing in front of me, standing in line the corner store. I follow the greasy thin combed sweep of hair from just above his left ear, rounding high his head, bald shining though the thinner it goes up and over, hair falling down to flip just above his right ear lobe. Fucking elegant. A masterpiece. How he does he do that? Why does he do that? I am too tired to think. An elderly lady the front of the line pays for her egg noodles in pennies. She counts them one at a time. Calling cards blazing trails of colors catch the impatient drift of my eye; they fall in a tumbling flurry on the wall behind the register, perhaps bright enough to keep my ass awake. Speed it up old lady, ain't got all night.

Out in the street yellow crowns of taxis scream me anywhere but here, they cut the misty street three lanes down Hyde, cutting like sharks one lane to another, tires wet on the pavement, headlights a blur in their coming. Just for the hell of it I want to raise my hand and hail, but I really do not know where I would go even if I could; home is where I am headed, the opposite direction up the hill. Still I am pulled by Veteran's, Luxor, and Yellow with their fluorescent advertisements; Fisherman's Wharf, ACT Theater, Cancun, a bottle of Seagram's, Prudential Life Insurance. I want to get away but one more block is ahead before I turn into the spiral of rights; right on O'Farrell, right into my building, right into the elevator, right down the hall, right through my front door and right into bed. My shoulders rise to the cold, I flip my hoodie up. Another taxi, another Cancun, it must be popular this time of year, never been there, everywhere else in Mexico but never Cancun, don't much care for touristy destinations. My mind goes drifting across the Caribbean to the warm beaches of past adventures, Puerto Rico, Jamaica, my last vacation; Dominican Republic, I am there without thinking.

TWENTY-SEVEN

We are puzzle pieces with tattered edges, worn from too many times being put together and pulled apart, too many attempts forcing ourselves into curves too small or too sharp. A week goes by and 'I love you' is the jump of my heart until Darnell calls and accuses me of plotting his assassination with the assistance of Kamala Harris. My door is then slammed shut, the phone not answered, his e-mails pour in at the speed of ten per day, delete, delete, delete. He appears on the street with the promise he's not stalking me, at my door ringing my phone to be let in, forgiven and forgotten, or outside Aunt Charlie's, a forever standing dive bar in the Tenderloin I drop into when I feel the need of people that care, people that don't see me in any other way than how I present in that moment. I have no story to them, no line of familiar, no image in their memory other than ordering a beer, a shot of Fernet, laughing and outwitting old fags, singing along with old school R&B on the juke box. Other than that, they have no idea who I am. They sit on their pickling stools just happy to see me. Darnell appears and appears again and all I gotta do is fall into those eyes of his, feel the whisper of his smile on my cheek or just sense the slight of his concern or care for me, our steps leading us through the streets or up the stairs into the mix of want and caution.

"Why is it every time we get in a fight you throw out my toothbrush?" Darnell stands with his face to the bathroom mirror, white teeth posing wide in an exaggerated stretch of open mouth. His eyes dash the whites quick for any flecks of food, he inspects his gums with two fingers lifting or dropping the pinch of his lips, sticks out his tongue. He spreads toothpaste on his dirty nailed fingertip hardly looking. I wonder why he doesn't just use my toothbrush. What makes a toothbrush a line so few dare to cross? I suck his dick and swallow his come, he chews the rosebud of my ass and tongues me as deep as he can, and then we kiss, mouths wide open, breathing each other's air, tongue rolling over tongue and teeth and yet sharing a toothbrush is a step just beyond reason. His paste covered finger jabs deep along his uppers and lowers. He spits. Opens wide. Inspects. Wipes his mouth with the back of his arm. Toothpaste still collects the corners of his mouth. How many times have I seen the end of him? How many times is never again? I wonder if Costco sells toothbrushes in bulk.

"Can I grab a couple of quarters?" He points to

the vintage coffee can I use for loose change. I nod and follow him a couple of steps so my presence won't allow for a handful to scoop into his pocket. It has happened before; a fist of coins fell from the cup of his hand into the deep of his pocket, then out the hole in the bottom. Spare change rolled the hardwood floors in every direction. He laughed. I frowned. Distrust is an anxious feeling. "Wanna buy some smokes." I nod. I step closer. I once bought him a pack, thinking it would stop him from diving into my quarters. Bought a pack of Basics or USA Gold's, cheap ass cigarettes, three twenty-five a pack, nothing like Marlboros or Camels. Six blocks later he had given most of the pack away to the endless, 'Hey bud, can I bum a smoke?' Darnell was king of the street for a minute. Mr. Generosity.

I hover in trepidation, look away insecure. My voice drops to just above a whisper, "Have you ever thought about getting on SSI?"

"What, you want your quarters back?" He turns and squares me in a challenge.

"No, I was just thinking that in between jobs ya might be able to get an income through SSI. Get your own place." I can't meet his eyes. I know there's no job to come.

"What, you don't like me staying here no more?"

"No, Darnell that's not what I am saying at all." I turn away; hide from the true of his words.

"Then why you askin'?" He walks to the window, back to me; he braces the edge of the desk in a lean, the line of his shoulders sexy in the stress and wide it becomes.

"Just thought your life might be a little bit easier . . ."

"What? With me outta yours? Is that what you're sayin'? Don't play me like Liza Minnelli!" I am so fucking transparent.

"I ain't playing you; I just want for you what is rightfully yours."

"What is rightfully mine ain't none of your business! All ya'all try and tell me what is right for me! I think for myself you know! I have two percent body fat and I burn hundreds of calories thinking for everyone else. I am tired of losing weight! No one thinks for their own fucking selves anymore! I gotta do it all!" I am swallowed sad in the thought of the echo chamber of his mind. Voices, real and imagined, the overwhelm of stimuli, lights, sirens, cars and buses, all that bouncing around in there without the ability to pause and determine where he begins and everything else ends. The insanity of the world dumps through him, the insanity of the world making him look like he is crazy. No wonder his fear is so high, his trust so low. He paces in circles; the kitchen, the living area, the bathroom and back again. He picks up a book, fans the pages, doesn't look at it, puts it down. Opens the refrigerator door, bends and reaches in, shuffles items on the racks but takes nothing out. He catches himself in a mirror, stops to make sure he is looking cool, is steady, adjusts his collar.

"I ain't no dependent on the system! No one here is supposed to take care of me! I take care of myself. I take care of myself and everyone else around here! Just like I always have! Don't pity my ass! I ain't got no reason to go on SSI!" The palm of his hand punches the wall.

"Darnell!" I tremble in the still of the room my shout has created. He stands in the archway of my entry hall. I push the words through the tight of my jaw. "I think it is time you looked into treatment." He looks at me with eyes teared and raging. "Schizophrenia." His stare deepens into me. "Get on some medication." He turns and faces the door.

His words are the blood of razors. "Don't try to make me fit into your idea of sanity." The drop of the deadbolt, the snap of the latch, the turn of the doorknob is the gun being loaded and now ready to fire. "Just remember, I ain't the crazy motha fucka who brings street scurryin' HIV-positive black boys home and feeds them cake!"

TENDER

PART TWO

ONE

I nurse my beer. I wanted to see Darnell today, saw him yesterday, seems like last week already. I didn't go though, couldn't stand the thought of standing in line in that cold stairway, thugs taking cuts, don't fuck with me attitudes, being hated for being white, hating being white, nothing I can do but steam like stew in my anger, wish county jail was more fucking organized, wish my world was somehow different, wish I had a shot of Fernet. Wanted to see Darnell the first glimpse of the blue skies at dawn until the spit of the sun got me depressed, rolled over after the alarm and went back to sleep. Maybe I'll order a shot.

Aunt Charlie's, a drag show, hair as high as the fucking ceiling, hips as narrow as the bar stools they sit. A benefit drag show, just like in the old days raising funds for struggling AIDS nonprofits just like bars used to do back in the day, early eighties when the government ignored our dying asses, when I waited days and weeks and months to die just like everyone else. And when I didn't I went looking for it, looking to die that is. Death by dick, fucked by infected men. Didn't work. Didn't die.

    Skinny trannies stroll in skirts skin thin. Two of them, flat hipped, side by side, four full cheeks rounding down below the hemlines, making their trannie stroll down the trannie bar. The fall of wigs shine synthetic colors unreal down their backs, the first the alarm of red, the other wavy blonde with streaks of darker shades, just like packaged amateur dye jobs of women in the suburbs. A large knuckled hand pats the wig perfect, deep lines run worn and weathered fingers; a second squared hand decked in bangles at the wrist glides over the shoulders of men lining the bar in her passing, while short strapped purses sway at the ends of long swinging arms, matching the pace of their casual indifference to the world.

    My phone vibrates, the same damn number as before. What the fuck, see who it is. "Hello."

    "I don't want your damn shot!" A queen down the bar screams my direction.

    "Hello?" The voice the other end of the line.

    "You can just fuck yourself!" The drag queen snarl continues.

    "Hello?" The voice, my phone, shouts my ear again.

    "Hello." I shout back. I plug my other ear with my finger. Gloria Gaynor screams the juke box as I head for the front door so I can hear this fucking call.

I will survive
Oh as long as I know how to love
I know I'll stay alive

"My name is Dianne Wright." I can barely hear this woman; the last name is striking familiar. "Hold on!" I shout into the phone dodging the dance of a desperately drunk old man, one arm waving the air in wide sweeps, the other planted to his swaying hips by the palm of his hand, his eyes closed, lips syncing, feeling the power of Gloria. I manage to get near the door.
"Hello!"
Silence sits the end of the phone. Then again in her unsteady, unsureness. "My name is Dianne Wright. I am calling regarding my son Darnell. You left a message with my daughter Debbie." I gape in a loss. What to say? "She passed on your number to me." My eyes search my mind. Her words are my nerves, trembling. "I haven't heard from my boy for two years now." Silence waters my eyes.
Dry mouth. Lips attempting to form words. "Perhaps soon" I mumble in my puddling discomfort. Caught I feel in wrong, drunk I am on Sunday afternoon. Fucking drunk. "Yea soon" I agree with myself. All I can manage.
"Soon?" She wanders in wonder.
"Darnell's in jail Mrs. Wright."
"Oh Lord, oh Lord . . ." In the pause I fall into visions of her bracing the chair, hand held to her heart. "Wwwwwhy . . . ?

"Possession of stolen property."

"Oh my child! My child!" Her voice carries away. I hate this. I fucking hate this shit.

"Sumptin' in my bones tole me sumptin' weren't right wit my boy. I tole his sister, cain't be good news someone else callin' on his behalf. How do you know my boy?" Mrs. Wright hits direct and hard. Almost an accusation, concern an echo softening any edge.

I struggle to speak. "I've been knowing him a year or more. We met, uh . . ." I can't shake the memory from its locked hiding place in my mind. "I, uh, met him in the subway. We hit it off, became friends . . . like immediately . . ." We fucked for two and a half hours I remember to myself. The best fuck I've ever had. "A year and a half ago we met." I repeat. "We dated for a while." Oh fuck! Does she know he's gay? I want to hang up, call her back.

"How long were you datin'?" Interest is peaked like my one eyebrow; my confidence is a half open doorway.

I try to count. "A few months." I count on fingers held in the air.

"That's not very long."

"Well things changed." I cringe to myself; we dated for a few months and have kept on fucking ever since.

"What you mean, changed? Did he change?"

"Excuse me?"

From the depths her words cut me. "I asked you, did Darnell change?"

I bleed in my memory of helplessness. "Yea." I stop. "Yea, something changed. He started to decline, started getting confused. I couldn't do anything. I couldn't help him. He needed help. I didn't know what to do. Mrs. Wright, are you aware Darnell has mental health issues?"

"Yes I know that Daniel." The sound of my name melts me like butter. We are suddenly face to face though a phone line reaching hundreds and hundreds of miles. The sound of my name and she and I are suddenly familiar, suddenly standing the same ground, suddenly speaking the same language. I am suddenly sober.

"Mrs. Wright, I honestly don't know what is going on." The flood is coming. "I mean, I know he is in jail, I know he has a court date in a couple of weeks, he says he was drugged with a rufie, he said he was asleep when he was arrested, I don't know what is fact and was is not . . ."

"Daniel, do you know he is bipolar?" Shaking my head to the ground, wrist pushing the tears back into my eyes it is then I notice her smooth. Her calm is the soft of Darnell's skin, her steady is the balance of his dancing feet on the wooden floors of my studio, her care is his hand taking mine in his, her words are his lips grazing my cheek whispering I love you.

"No Mrs. Wright, I didn't know that. I thought he was schizophrenic."

"He's been bipolar for twenty years now, Daniel. Just like his daddy. Bad blood from his daddy's side."

TWO

Orange is a color only suitable for fruit and warning signs I think to myself as men one by one file past the window, a couple in shackles, one in cuffs; a navy blue cop with a key follows to unlock the cuffed man once he reaches the phone. Brown skin each of them, hard eyes, proud chins, sexy as fuck, my desire drips.

"Sick of these macho attitudes in here." Darnell's eyes dagger side to side once he is allowed to sit and pull the receiver from the cradle. I stare into him praying his anxious mind will settle away from the others. I remember how it used to get stuck there, fixated on some trivial point for long stretches of time.

"There was a piece of glass outside your door, part of a crack pipe I am sure" he said one evening.

"Not mine. I don't smoke crack." His eyes were unconvinced.

"I know it was part of a pipe, and it was right outside your front door."

"It's not mine." My measured words slide sad. The same words would replay in a few hours, a couple of days, a week, the following month.

Behind the glass Darnell tries to gather himself, distracted he faces me, shoulders square, mumbles down his rant. "Macho like they got shit to prove." Eyes meeting mine then cornering the men sitting either side. He continues. "Who the fuck cares?" He stands, puts one foot up on his stool, slides his hand along his elastic waistline and dives deep into his crotch. His chin challenges me. So bad I wish my hand was down the front of my jeans. "They all got nine inches, ten inches, eleven . . ."

THREE

I stand in the shower shaving my pubes. I don't know why I bother. I shave my pubes because every man walking through my front door shaves his. It makes their dicks look like raw untamed primordial appendages; the arm of their flaccid arching just that much more minus the engulfing stash of hair at the base causing the rocket of their erection to aggress longer, harder, and with definitive aim. Fewer pubes make for fewer pauses while giving a man head, annoyances of pulling hair from my teeth, the inside of my cheek, hair tickling the back of my throat coughing me a gag reflex, hair the tip of my tongue rather than the hard dirty lines I want to shove at him. "Come on baby, give me that dick!"

It takes a long painstaking time shaving my pubes. No nicks. No gashes. No raw skin from repetitive passes. Pay attention to every move. One slight slip of the blade could wreck sex for a week. The urgency to pee weighs heavy. Lifting the razor I pause before allowing myself the luxury of letting go as I smile back some thirty four years. At sixteen I peed in the shower for the very first time, a freedom I had never known. I laughed when I peed, it felt so fucking good. It was the same year I was allowed to stay out till midnight on Friday and Saturday nights. The freedom of yellow foam frothing the drain was the freedom to wander the maze of streets in Val Vista, my neighborhood; 1970's single story California white stucco tract homes. Ranch style they called them, every fourth house ugly identical, small yards, tight fences, windows staring into neighboring windows, no fucking ranch as far as I could see just swarms of tract homes, a ranch of ugly houses if you ask me. I recall peeing in the shower, the burn of thirty-four years ago, memories of wandering those streets draining me.

FOUR

"I wait six and a half days for this twenty minute visit."

Darnell's eyes trail slow; his grasping the receiver of the phone between us, the length of the cord leading him to me, his lift to my waiting smile, his sudden smile, his drifty eyes trying to lift his smile for real. Something is wrong, something is different. Where has the reckless command of his existence gone? How does mania turn soft and sensitive and dull? They dosed him with something I tell myself. We sit for a moment. His eyes drift beyond me, back to me, to the side of me. "Are you alright?"

"Yea." From a dream his hand rubs his backside. "They gave me a shot."

"A shot of what?"

"Haldol." The word punches the wind out of me.

Horse tranquilizer. My mouth opens, no words come. I want to bite the receiver of the phone.

Our conversation dulls me like Klonopin and beer. Minutes are sluggish until the guard appears the end of the row of orange jumpsuits. The overhead lights flash on and off to signal the end of twenty fucking minutes.

"I love you . . ." Darnell waits for my return of love. Rage begins to gather in me.

"I love you too baby . . ." The phones saddle themselves. I stand as slow as Darnell's trace in the world. "Horse tranquilizer." I anger my words in my turn. "Horse tranquilizer." I find myself stumbling. "HE AIN'T NO ANIMAL!!!" My words bounce off the glass back. My thumb clenched fists pound my thighs. "He ain't no animal." I mumble. The other visitors stare me down. I don't have to look at them to feel them shake their heads in their turn away. Orange is a blur trailing my right eye through my left and is gone.

I wish I would show up one Saturday only to have the jailer say, 'He was released this morning.' After three months of hearing Darnell's promise 'I will be out in a couple weeks, my lawyer says so,' after three months of endless Friday redialing the jail number to make a reservation, after three months of calling Dianne and protecting her with half truths, 'Your son is fine . . .' my heart grows impatient. Just get him the fuck off Haldol! Just get him the fuck outta here! In the meantime we wait. I call, I write, I visit, we hope, we gaze into each other, we wait some more.

The Plexiglas between us seems more yellow today than in previous visits. We sit for a moment.

Sometimes nothing to say falls between us as it does now. Instead of an intimidating distance our eyes bleed into each other, wading along the edge of discomfort to a reassuring ground of content at just being able to see one another.

"You never mention your dad. Where's he at?" I gentle the words between us. A question I already know the answer to from conversations with his mother but want to hear from him.

"My daddy left us when I was seven." Darnell replies with eyes rolling, then resting. I kick myself for asking. I did not mean to down him. Saliva pools inside his parted lower lip, the brink of a drool but instead his lips close, he breathes the spit into a deep swallow, a sucking sound as the back of his wrist wipes his mouth. "My sisters were raised and outta the house by then. It was just my mama and me, sometimes my nephew, I'd baby sit him."

My week ago memory calls back my last phone conversation with his mother. "I can still see my boy in the garage with his daddy. He was four or five. Uh, uh, uh. The two of them cleaning the garage together, both them with man size brooms and there go my boy trying to imitate his daddy, trying to keep up with his daddy's sweepin'." Dianne chuckles, eyes probably sparkling tears with that memory. "No, that boy of mine could not keep up with his daddy. That broom was four times bigger than he was. He tried every which way. He tried swingin' it, pushin' it, draggin' it..." Dianne's chuckles deepen. I wonder if her tears are of laughter or loss or just fond of a long ago time. "His daddy stood there over his boy, big ole hands overlapping his small fisted grips on that broom. His daddy pushin' that broom with his only boy. Pushin' it back and forth, back and forth. They was cleanin' that garage together." Dianne's voice drifts into silent memories.

I pull myself out of that garage, away from a memory not my own. Darnell's voice dulls through the line. "The last time I spoke to him was fifteen years ago when I graduated from Junior College in Southeast Texas. He called to tell me he couldn't make it to the graduation. He was too busy." The receiver of the phone drops away with the weakening of his words, the yellow Plexiglas seems to dim. "He was always too busy." I struggle imagining so many years not speaking with my father. The distance between my father and me can't be measured in miles or time, best measured in our differences. I push myself once a month to make the call to him to just check in, all the while knowing it will last five minutes. After all, you can only talk about the weather for so long.

Dianne's and my conversation continues in the back of my mind. "Back thirty or so years Darnell's daddy, come to find out, was jumpin' in and outta bed with nearly every woman 'tween here and Dallas." Dianne sighs regret or disgust, I am not sure. "Uh, uh, uh. That man sure had an appetite." She sighs again.

Darnell wipes his forehead with the orange length of his forearm, wipes again the threat of drool the corner of his mouth. "My daddy accused my mama of foolin' around behind his back." His head shakes. "In fact when I was about to be born he denied being the father." Sad I feel as his stare narrows the initial-etched shelf I rest my elbows on, Darnell not able to lift his eyes to meet mine. "It wasn't till I was born my daddy showed up in the hospital and claimed me. Claimed me like covering up a mistake or something. Claiming me like a lost article of clothing. Naming me after him. His boy. His son. His blood." I kick myself again for the down topic I brought up. "So much for being his namesake. Don't hardly know nothing about the man."

Dianne's voice jumps back my mind. "That's how I come to find out Darnell's daddy was bipolar. Mania they said often comes sexually." Oh shit. My mind wanders from Dianne's meandering stroll through her story to my own sexual appetite. How close am I to mania? Bipolar. The countless men; the insatiable desire. "The straw that broke the camel's back was when he was seein' the lady 'cross the back alley." The phone shuffles at her end. "Lord have mercy. Her husband came home and found the two of them. My husband sailed out their back door and over our backyard fence landin' on the edge of the above ground swimmin' pool." Dianne pauses before she laughs. "That man smashed the side of that pool and water flooded the entire backyard! The neighbor's yard too! That was a big pool!" Laughter overtakes her, she stops for a breath. "Chlorine killed everything in its path! Every plant, every bug, every blade of grass . . . ." Her laughter wanes as the picture she paints comes clear in my mind. I notice I am smiling hard despite the tragedy of the story. "He left shortly thereafter."

Darnell and I stare into one another. Give it a rest I think to myself. No more stupid questions. "Why do you hate your father?" Darnell's question is like a sudden voice in a fuzzy dream, the annoying wallow of a prodding therapist. I open my open eyes as if they were closed as Darnell waits for my response.

"What makes you think I hate my father?"

Darnell's face pushes closer to the glass. "Anything you have ever said about him is negative. His lies, his abuse, his many wives. You even said once he likes your brothers more than he likes you . . . you being gay and all. Is that why you hate him?" I don't recall ever talking to Darnell about my father. I shake my attempt to remember, recognize his fixation, face his question eye to eye hoping to ease his attention.

"I don't hate him." I wonder in a flash if I love him. "He had an affair while my mother lay in a coma dying in the hospital." I see my father and his affair sitting on my mother's couch smoking cigarettes and drinking scotch. Ugly, the two of them, fucking ugly. "Marriage to that woman was imprinted in his mind long before his wife, my mother, was even fucking ashes in a box." I notice the rise in my voice. "He shamed my brothers and me!" I look to the visitors afraid they might overhear me. I bow my head embarrassed but feeling the red of my rising anger. He sat on the edge of my bed and said, "Don't judge me until you have walked a mile in my footsteps." I bite. "Some fucking justification."

"So you hate him . . ." Darnell's eyebrows lift.

"Time's up! Visiting is over!" The world stops in my last eye meeting of Darnell.   Lights flashing.

Our hands rise to peace signs through the pale Plexiglas. Too short a visit. Darnell in line with the others. A five year old boy with a big ole broom. A young man growing into his father.

"I ain't so different from my own..." I mumble to him through the soundproof glass as my step carries me through the tall barred gate.

FIVE

    Sirens scream the streets, St Francis Hospital is in a mood beckoning the weak and weary and fragile of spirit. It is there, behind me, high upon Nob Hill where the Tenderloin bury their dead, or so it seems. Tombs of the penniless quick my imagination, a potter's field in the bowels of St Francis, I laugh at my absurdity but cry for the fruitful lives having died alone in antiseptic hospital rooms monitored by graveyard shift nurses wearing thick soled shoes under the shine of fluorescent white. Yet sirens do not scream when paramedics carry corpses from the Tenderloin hotels or apartment buildings, a hush rushes the block while we, the stoopers of the street, watch the red lights flashing, pulling away without a word to anyone. The grief of our eyes are silent as they go. I see the dead just before they die pushing themselves along in the streets, wheelchairs, walkers and canes; self propelled by the labor of the wind in their breath, the need of the moment, the change from a dollar rattling in their hands; a bottle of soda, a single cigarette, bananas moaning of their bruises. They stand the line of Glide's soup kitchen, St Anthony's, the senior centers, their efforts for a meal a labor of hours. Bone thin faces, eyes dull like worn pennies, bones pushing through gray skin no matter their pallor; brown is gray, gold is gray, white is gray, gray is the stench of yesterday and the tedious days before. They sell their Meals on Wheels for a dollar on the sidewalk down at the corner.

SIX

    My Therapist asks, "Why don't you volunteer somewhere?"
    My Doctor asks, "Why don't you take a trip somewhere?"
    My Psychiatrist asks, "Why don't you go stay with your family for awhile?"
    And my father asks every goddamn time I call, "Why don't you just go back to work?"
    Pacing is a well worn path in my studio; the bed, the bathroom, the kitchen, the couch, the window, the bed, pathways of anxious pacing. I pace before having to leave to see my therapist, pace before going to corner store, pace before pushing laundry down the block, pace every goddamn time I had to leave for any goddamn reason. When I'm not pacing I am under the covers waiting for them to be lifted again

so the light of life can shine my step one more time.

"How long have you known Darnell?" Marilyn's efficient pen is ready to note anything I say; I can hear ink burn the page through the phone connection.

"About a year and a half."

"And what is your relationship to him?"

"Friend."

"He said lover." If you knew, then why the fuck ask? I wonder. Still punched breathless I am. My open mouth cannot agree or disagree. Flattered, but in a snap ashamed; hopeful, but in a breath afraid; coupled, but in a slap alone.

"If," my words fail my thoughts, "If I am his lover," I pause, "I am a cautious one."

"What do you mean by that Mr. Hill?"

"I, I, I mean I don't know what his illness is. I, I don't know if he can recover. I don't know how he will be when he gets out. I don't know if I can deal . . ." Words and thoughts and explanations run into one another but I am dumbed.

"He is schizoaffective; he has no insight into his behavior . . ." My hand reaches through the phone and grabs Marilyn's throat.

"How insightful can a person be when they are doped up on Haldol?"

"Mr. Hill, the psychiatrist has diagnosed and prescribed the medication appropriate for his condition."

"Have you met Darnell?" My question is more an accusation.

"Yes Mr. Hill I met him once."

"Once?"

"Yes once."

"How often does he see the Psychiatrist?"
"The Psychiatrist has seen him once."
"Once?"
"Yes once." I count on my hand the number of weeks Darnell has been in jail, the number of weeks the drool of Haldol drowns his words into a tunnel of short thoughts, dumbs his brilliant mind into dull and empty. I can't count past three, my rage screams counting impossible.

SEVEN

I peer across the street into the apartment of an elderly Chinese couple. She stands at the stove stirring in a frying pan with quick revolutions while her other hand lifts and jerks the pan over the flame. He steps around her, patting her backside gently as he goes, sits on a stool in the window in his pajama bottoms and T-shirt. He places his slippered foot in the sill of the window, lights a cigarette, and blows smoke in a large round billow into the air.

EIGHT

    Alone in the elevator at 850 Bryant going up seven floors yet again to county jail, I pick my nose in the slow brightly lit lift. I hate this fucking place, rakes my very last nerve. I get here early to be the first in line. I am silent in my picking, determined to clean my burning nostrils of the dry poppered snot from last night. Fucking can't stand this place rolls my mind over and over. As the elevator comes to a slow stop I jump as I realize I am probably being watched on someone's camera. Fuck you I mumble as I face the ceiling to see if the camera is there in the corners, behind the panels, under the light. Fuck you. They must have cameras all over this fucking place, elevators, stair wells, hallways, even in the fucking john I bet. Maybe I should go jack in the fucking john, give these assholes something to watch. The doors open, I pull my hand away quickly and make like I am wiping something off my face.

"Your mom put our names in her prayer circle at church." Darnell's shaking forehead plants into his cupped palm. His face lifts the other side of the Plexiglas, a smile sweeps with the roll of his eyes. So rare I see him smile anymore. "It was hard getting her off the phone. Shit! That woman can talk." Darnell's smile brightens as he slowly comes around. He is so beautiful right this second. To hold this moment, just to hold this moment, but the twenty minute clock ticks away. "Hey Darnell," I step softly, "I spoke with Jail Psyche this week."

"What did they have to say?" Sarcasm questions as bright as the orange seat suit draping him.

"Miss Marilyn Sanders says ya gotta be more forthcoming about your drug use and manic episodes." Sarcasm meets sarcasm hoping I don't drop a heavy on him.

"What drug use?" I realize I don't have a clue what I am talking about. I have only seen him high a couple of times, maybe a few in the year and a half I have known him. My heart searches for the right direction, the right tone to carry my meaning. In my pause the twenty minute clock is ticking.

"Whatever drugs you have done."

"I ain't a drug addict."

"I think they want you to be one." The tilt of Darnell's head registers confused. How do I say what I wanna say? Just fucking say it. "If you have a drug problem they can place you easier than if you don't." Darnell's puzzle floats the air between us, his eyes searching for reason. I breathe short before I punch, "If ya ain't got a fucking drug problem Darnell, get one." I aim my intensity into him; his attention is a moving target. Eyes meet mine, he nods slow, nods some more with his shoulders and chest as my words sink in. I stare into the phone in my hand, hearing the recorded voice each time it is lifted from its cradle, 'This call is subject to monitoring and recording.' Great. Do they really listen? Just fucking great. Fuck 'em, I think, fuck 'em.

Where do I go from here? "Do you remember the night you thought I was Robert Downey Jr.?" Darnell's nonstop rambling kept me up until four in the morning all the while insisting I needed to have a tighter rein on my royalties, needed to take accounting classes to budget myself more efficiently, needed to see psychotherapists to practice boundary setting, at one point grabbing my forearms angrily, pinning my arms across my chest and insisting I call my agent that very minute.

"I do remember that." His guard walls high between us.

Carefully I continue, "Do you remember I had to trick you out of the building by saying we were going to my agent's?" He nods unable to look at me. "Once outside I turned back into the building leaving you out in the cold, locking you out. Do you remember that?" My tears threaten, the question pleads.

Darnell's eyes lift to mine. "I do." Pain fills his eyes, skinny eyebrows narrow. I wonder if that is shame in his shadow, please don't be ashamed.

"What was that like for you?" My hands shake. My breath jumps.

Darnell does not answer, does not appear as if he is going to. A minute passes. "It's hard to explain," is almost a whisper. "Headaches." He mumbles. "Scared." He turns away. I let him rest, discomfort quiets. I press nothing. "I couldn't stop the voices. I couldn't stop my mind from thinking so fast . . ." He won't turn back to me. His ear still listening into the receiver of the phone. I wait.

"Hey. Hey." He turns slowly back. "Just tell them that, tell those Jail Psyche people that. If you can't think of it in sentences just write down words that describe it." Darnell's eyes run red the rims. "Baby, if you are gonna get out of here they have to feel like there is something they can do to help you, send you somewhere to get that help. Get it? Give them something they think they can fix." His bowed head nods. Twenty minutes nearly gone.

I don't want to push anymore. I can't change the subject to something like the fucking weather. The Plexiglas seems gray. My fingers follow the carved initials L.W.J. It seems I always choose the same booth each visit. Who is L.W.J.? I feel Darnell's eyes on me before I hear his words. "I'm sorry for all I put you through." I look away, shake my head. My arms ache to hold him. Life without justice. L.W.J.

NINE

Steps climb but I can't. Gray weathered planks past the age of old, faded layers of blue gray paint chipping away feed the stab of my week-long anxiety with their years of wear and weariness. Seven months and some odd days brought me here; I stopped counting last week when Marilyn Sanders's words were welcome for the first time. "Darnell will be released on Tuesday." I froze then like I freeze now standing with the wind blowing my back. 'Thanks' was all I could mutter. She gave me the address, a few blocks from the projects in the Fillmore. I contemplated a cold beer, a shot of Fernet but it was just a quarter after nine in the morning, too early, uncivilized, a couple hours later it would be a different story. My limits are fucking laughable, I thought to myself. So I had a shot, saved the beer for later.

Waiting has been forever, this day too long in coming. Never knowing Darnell's exact release date from jail has been a countdown to zero, an ambiguous tally of days we are not together. Steps climb the front of this towering old Victorian; a deep breath to gather my heart back into my chest, a brief pause to allow the tears to rain inside of me rather than out the corners of my eyes and down along my cold winded cheeks. Can't have Darnell see me weak. I wait until I can count to ten and swallow full without it getting stuck in my throat. Gotta be strong, gotta be strong, my man is waiting, gotta be strong and up I go, step by step.

Flat opens the door; Flat as in no expression. He is tall, skinny, white and dreadlocked. Red pimples litter his cheeks, more skin than hair beards his chin and jaw line. I take another deep breath; dreads never look right on white people I think as I ensure my eyes don't roll when I meet his questions. The tilt of his head sizes me up. "Can I help you?" come the words but I swear I didn't see his lips move. He must be a counselor; a rehab like this place has got to have a guard dog like that at the door.

"My name is Daniel; I called earlier about Darnell Wright." Flat doesn't seem to register my words at first, must be sinking through the mud of his mind.

His face nods, his dreads don't move. "Hold on."

The door is closed; I turn as my eyes fall down the steep stumble of stairs I just climbed. In my wait I see Dianne stirring by her phone, nerved to joy to hear the lost voice of her boy, the voice gone missing for two years now. I promised her we would call. "It will be the first thing we do" I lied knowing full on the first thing Darnell and I will do is hold the real of each other in our hands, smell the soft of skin in our embrace, whisper 'I love you' just loud enough to know it is not a dream. Waiting, I wonder if we will have a minute alone. Waiting I wonder when we will be able to spend the night together. Cigarette butts overflow a tall cylinder ashtray at my side, each a story of waiting, waiting to detox, waiting for the desire to use again, waiting on a visitor or family member with unwavering faith coming to visit, one last drag waiting to stride back into life and give it another shot.

The wind opens the door, Flat extends his dead arm in a half baked welcome. "Come in."

"Thanks." I step the threshold into the living room.

"He'll be right here." Flat's lips still don't move. I lower the backpack I brought for Darnell to the floor. Flat eyes it, eyes me, eyes the bag again, twenty something and skeptical like an old dog. Darnell has nothing I realized when I hung up with Marilyn last week; it's not the first time he hasn't had anything, I told myself. So I packed underwear, socks, t-shirts, jeans, thermals, a hoodie, razors, shaving cream, toothbrush and paste; my list ran long, from nothing to something are many lines on a pad of paper. He might not ever use this shit. He might just up and leave, flee the program, flee the city, flee my sorry ass. I drift. The last items packed were small cans of apple juice. Darnell loves cold apple juice in the morning. Me and my coffee, him and his juice, some morning soon I hope.

Flat keeps eyeing the backpack as if it contains

contraband. "Clothes for Darnell." Flat checks the bag again. "Toiletries ya know." Flat eyes me. I wonder into his eyes what does it take to make this fucker talk? "The backpack is mine." I balance it more solid against the side of a couch. His silence nerves me into talking. "I lived out of it for six and a half years when I was on the road." I feel Flat's eyes on me more curious but I stare into the bag with memories. His silent distrust of me is a slow nail down the chalk board so I play for empathy knowing this rehab is for folks with HIV, psyche issues and substance abuse. I also know Rehab counselors are the closed or open doors between me and my man. No more fucking cops, no more fucking Plexiglas. Gotta keep it real. Gotta pity myself to get respect.

"Back in eighty-nine they told me I had two years to live, told me there was no cure for AIDS. So I quit doing drugs, quit drinking, gave up all I owned, packed some clothes in that bag and headed north." Flat's eyes and mine meet. He almost smiles, a glimpse of familiar, an almost 'I get it.' "Traveled like a gypsy with my bag on my back every step of the way, the woods of Oregon, the rain forests of Hawaii, the castles of Prague, the ruins of the Andes, the streets of Oakland, all over the fucking place." Flat's eyes are less skeptical, still his sealed lips keep his pimples in place. I brush a swatch of dirt off the bag as if to pride it with dignity as my memories wander into slower reflections. "I worked with orphans in Guatemala, on reforestation projects in Hawaii, with ex-cons in North Carolina." My mind drifts to a path long ago lost; a path of justice and compassion in the world and to think my life has come to dick and beer. "It's Darnell's journey now," I pat the bag, "it starts with the basics."

"Nice." Flat pushes a slow bounce up from his belly, his eyebrows high arches as he leans against the banister of the stairs and crosses one leg over the other. I smile at finally reaching the dog of him.

The living room is a long exhale, high ceilings, bright windows, three beige couches curling the shape of a U, a big screen TV commanding the end, a large black hole so easy to fall into. The air is stale, still, quiet, a shut in feeling, oppressive despite the sunny windows. Open this shit up; let that wind bring life back into this place. The stairway climbs to the second floor, my eyes rise to the dark landing above. "No guests allowed." Flat points with his head up the stairs.

"Can I sit down?" I drop heavy without waiting his response. I don't know why I sit, been sitting all day. Nerves I guess. Should have had a beer with that shot of Fernet before coming, the edge of this place is awkward, this ride a little too fucking sober and Flat is too much fucking effort.

I don't recall standing but here I stand. I don't recall stepping but my feet round the end of the couch. I don't recall Flat leaving but he is nowhere to be seen. Darnell and I swim through the air in three quick strokes, arms swallowing the short between us until the warm smooth of Darnell's cheek brushes mine, pillows mine. Real is a dream I will wake into in a breath, real is not this body pressing against mine, this soft chest, the roll and cush of this belly, the wide of these hips and thighs hindered by layers of clothes. Real is not these empty searching hands up and down my back, not this unsteady mind of mine worrying if hugging my man is allowed in rehab or if they will step in to pull us apart. Real is not my drained lover pushing through the motions two beats after the thought. If this was real the silence would not be screaming me deaf like it is, I would hear the loud longing of our desire, the groan of I miss you, the chatter of how good you look, how sweet you feel. But silence is the trouble of words I drown in. Nothing seems to fit, a foot too big for a shoe, a hat too small for a head, a ring too tight for a fat knuckled finger but still my mind searches, looking for a way to slide it on, searching for the words to make the shock of today, the shock of our discomfort right and good for at least just right now.

 My sudden erection shatters uncertainty and I bury my face there in the curve of his neck, there under the spread of his hollow palm on the back of my head, there in the heavy perspiring smell of my man. My hands search through the layers. Gone is the washboard tummy, the twenty-eight inch waist, gone is the hard muscle dense of biceps and chest, gone is the confidence that carried it all. My stomach heaves to cry but I pull in tight and hold my breath. "Oh baby" is all I can say, all I can repeat until words are useless and the search for them vain. My lips mouth his neck, lifting to his cheek, finding his lips open and daring. Deep is not deep enough, want never filled and never going to be filled; begging I am only to pull away against the drive of our seven month dream as Flat steps our direction down the hall. Pulled away, our watered eyes sadden. He'll come back I convince myself. He'll come back; the swift of his thoughts and wit, the charge of his conquest, the tight of his dancer's body. He'll come back.

Darnell's hands tremble as I hand him the open cell phone with Dianne's number dialing. He backs his wrist to his mouth, sucks the drool deep his throat, a straw draining the bottom of the glass. His eyes bulge, more whites than the shining round gems of caramel I know. So dull they seem. "Hello mama..." I take his other hand, his grip has no hold, his hand simply rests in mine. "Yes mama I am doing fine." The long silences between his short responses leave me thinking Dianne's words must be nailing him to the cross that hangs over her bed. Twenty minutes pass, must be a fucking sermon.

"It's time my boy become a man. You can tell him that." Dianne shouts my memory from our first conversation. But as Darnell's tears begin to fall I recall the strength of her direction, the tender of her hope, the mind of her prayers, the true of her love.

"Dinner!" comes a shout from the kitchen. "Dinner's ready!" Into the living room step her words before she emerges from the hall. Old, but not the truth of old. Street old. Drug old. The damage of a hard life. Wrinkles run her face, dark rings bag her eyes, lines cut her lips while the dance of forty is in her eyes, not the sixty she is looking. Claw hands at the ends of wiry arms, brown hands in a white frayed towel passing over each, more nervous than efficient. In a softer voice, more polite, "Dinner."

"Thanks." I smile.

"You the new one?" She aims my direction. "I was the new one two weeks ago." White towel on her hip waits for a response.

"No, I'm-a, I'm just visiting."

"What about him? He the new one?"

I look sideways at Darnell hoping he will respond. His eyes ask what the fuck. My head nods her way.

"My name is Darnell."

"Hey sweetheart, come get some dinner." The white towel waves her direction in the air. "You come too." I hesitate, not sure if staying is alright. "You can stay for dinner. I cook a lot of food. I like big appetites." The white towel waves again. "All us have visitors some time or another stayin' for dinner." The white towel waves in the air pointing upstairs to where the residents sleep, down the hall where the kitchen and dining room are, back and forth over her head. "Come have some dinner. Oh yea sweetheart, my name is Bernice." In her sharp turn to the kitchen I see how her flat chest pushes her through her world, her bony ass sticking out far behind. "We always have visitors . . ." her words turn down the hall. "That's why I make so much food. Come to think of it, I been here two weeks and I haven't had a visitor . . ." Darnell and I stand. I don't want to go home but I know he has to be on his own right now.

"I'm not staying for dinner baby." The tears I have been swallowing this past hour with him will soon be raging. But not in front of these people, not in front of Darnell. His rise to me is a slow mechanical effort. His wide eyes beg me to stay. "But I will be here for you every step of the way, whatever it takes to get you through this baby, every fucking step of the way."

    I walk Darnell to the kitchen. A line of mostly men, five or six, another woman, wraps around an island in the center of the kitchen, each holding a plate with white latex gloved hands. "Sweetheart get your gloves on." Bernice hands Darnell a pair. "Sanitary purpose. In the kitchen eatin' your food, ya always gotta be wearin' 'em." She smiles a wide closed mouth smile deepening the lines in her brown skin. Darnell turns to me holding the gloves between two fingers. I feel his pain, the length of his 'Oh no, ya gotta be kidding.'

    I look him square in the eye before I pivot to go, "Every step of the way."

TEN

My head bows to the gray of the pavement beneath my step. For one block I find solace there, follow the lines and cracks in the sidewalk. I roll with the blow of trash; a brown paper bag hugging a beer can, bright orange Cheetos tossed to the pigeons, rectangles of shiny silver Wrigley's wrappers, stained napkins and paper coffee cups, greased and cheesy foil from a burrito flips in the breeze. My nerve leaps from staring into the stains of dried bird shit to rounds of flattened black gum long chewed, spit and ground into the pavement. The crawl of wrinkled fingers with dirt black nails pick up cigarette butts to salvage the last drags of tobacco. Boots, old sneakers and house slippers quick step a pair of canary yellow Pumas, bright navy blue jeans bagging the legs. Folded green dollars jump hand to hand. Yellow Pumas rolls his in a wad. It doesn't take a lift of my eyes to complete the dealer's picture. At the corner my chin raises to know. Is it red or is it green? Do I stop? Do I go?

    Trust is a word spray painted under a window three flights up at the Page Hotel, corner of Turk and Leavenworth; red paint dripping like blood over old yellow bricks, all in thick lettered caps, the R is backwards. Fuck trust, I think to myself walking along, aiming for the bus to take me to Darnell in rehab. Faces of friends fall in my mind like dominos as I search for someone I can trust, someone I can call, someone who would tell me honestly if I was out of my mind dating a man fresh out of jail, fresh into rehab, then again I ask myself, is it trust or is it the truth I am afraid to hear. I am fucking crazy. The last domino falls. "Fuck trust." I spit the words into the passing traffic. "Ain't no one I can trust!" My own words catch my surprise as I look left and then right. A pair of old sad watery eyes meet mine in a rush of passing by, they drop away indifferent. Only in the Tenderloin can you talk to yourself like this and no one pays you serious mind, I think to myself, catching myself, chuckling I'm just as crazy as half the mother fuckers on this block. Shit. I take a step with my head tilted up at the window trying to imagine who the hell would hang out their window upside down to spray paint the word trust. Desperate, delusional, drug addicted. It is open, the window that is, I slow to see if someone passes by to get an eye on who did it, no one does, the empty window sits black with billowing purple curtains. Trust. Sometimes I wish I had one beer drinking buddy I could talk to, woe to, tell my sad story of Darnell to. The dominos fall again. The white full moon sits in the pale afternoon sky just over the roof of the Hotel Hurly across the street. Full moon at noon, shit, no wonder my ass is so damn horny. Got to get to Darnell. My mind rushes my feet to move. Our first free day together; Darnell on a pass from rehab, I gotta get moving.

"How is it dating me in this tunnel?" Outside rehab, at the top of the stairs Darnell points with an orange Bic lighter to the side of his head.

"Fine!" I can't even focus on his words at first because all I have in mind is to get him home and get him fucking. We tumble down the stairs, flame, smoke, the air of tobacco and a deep drag off a white butt. Direct is not something I do so well especially with a question I'd never expect. Darnell looks at me with a yea right eyebrow. "Fine." I feel my eyebrows ascend to my scalp in my pushed up smile. Stupid fuck I am. I feel like a squeaky clean red headed cheerleading teenage girl with freckles and braces, pony tails pulled tight, blue and gold pompoms dancing in the air. Everything is F-I-N-E, fine. I choke. The fade of Darnell's words repeat themselves at least three times over in my mind. Dang, surprise the shit out of me. Hit me when I wasn't looking. For the first time in seven and a half months Darnell looks deeply into me, sees right through me as if my lie can be read behind the blue of my eyes. "It's hard." I humble the truth in the two soft stumbling words. I keep my eyes on him. "But I know there is life beyond this shit Haldol and it is just going to take some time. You're coming along man." My arm reaches around his shoulder. "Each week they take you down a notch on Haldol and up a notch on that other shit."

"Lamictal."

"Yea, Lamictal." Darnell's attention is straight ahead not even trying to meet my eyes. I fear I lost his trust in me. "We gotta have faith." I stop in our wander to face him square.

"You sound like my mother." He soft hits me the back of his hand.

I laugh a "fuck you" at him. His smile shines a quick bright and then fades into the cold December sidewalk. Maybe I didn't lose him after all.

Silence carries us from one corner to the next. "Really though, you gotta be patient with this shit, meds are nothing to mess with. It takes time baby, it really takes time." I pause in my hypocritical babble recalling how I had no patience for my own meds to land. Shit, look at me now, stupid hypocritical cheer leader. "Trust baby, trust."

"What makes it hard?" Darnell keeps his eye on the approaching bus stop; the 38 Geary from the Fillmore to the Tenderloin is a direct line from rehab to my bed. My pace slows with my thoughts. How do I tell a man he isn't picking up his end of the conversation? How do I tell a man his one word answers leave me desperate to make decisions? What's up? Nothing. What do you want to do? Whatever. What do you want to eat? No word but shrugging shoulders. How do I tell my man I long to know what is inside his mind without picking at it like a fucking bird pulling worms from the mud? How do I tell him? The bus arrives, we curl into the line. I lean into Darnell.

"I miss your poetry."
"Not inspired."
"We don't talk like we used to. You don't volunteer your ideas like you used to. I miss that."
Weaving our way through the thick stand of bodies I hear the bus driver shout, "Move to the back of the bus! Come on! We got people wanting to get on board here!" Darnell and I grab hold of the overhead rail, silver, cold. "Well it's like you said, it's gonna take time." His reply seems pat. I wish he would disagree or have his own damn thought about it.
We ride the crowded bus lost in our own crowded thoughts. The blank faces around us appear lost in their own. Darnell stares. His stare is slow. I wonder if he is up for sex. I wonder how I will look myself in the mirror afterwards knowing I gave my ass to a crazy motherfucker. But I did when he was ranting and screaming in the streets, pacing my apartment thinking I was Robert Downey Jr. I argue myself. Fuck I don't know. Is he crazy or am I? I go back to a long ago night, Darnell ranting about medications. His image flashes my memory like a stuttering black and white movie. He stood at the end of the bed nearly shaking in his anger. "They put me on Lithium one time, then Depakote, and then fucking Wellbutrin! That shit's for crazy people!" I wondered how he sees himself. "I got so freaked out on Depakote I had to go to the hospital and beg to get my stomach pumped!" Uneasy I became hearing his retelling. I saddened into sympathy and held him until those memories of his dissolved into that long ago night. We fell asleep for the first time, and perhaps the only time, with his

head on my chest, his arms wrapping the bones of my ribs. Tight, so tight, it was as if he was afraid to let go.

    The bus slows as the huge glaring concrete white of the Catholic Archdiocese begs heads to turn its direction. Two rows of Latina women sitting beneath us in seats cross themselves as the bus passes. Darnell watches unmoved, clinging to the rail overhead, casually wiping drool from the corner of his mouth on the sleeve of his extended arm. I consider Darnell through the reach of our arms overhead, hands holding the long silver bar, belly hiding under layers, a thermal, a sweater, a jacket. I notice his wide stance bracing him as the bus leans the curve of O'Farrell, his muscular thighs nearly busting the seams of his khakis. Naked on my mind, heavy in my eyes, wondering how am I gonna handle the drool.

    Sex is slow. I can count the cracks in the ceiling but I will do him no dishonor. I smell his masculine instinct falter in his awakening. This too will take time. Sex is quick. Twenty minutes, maybe thirty. Two hours of his attention is what my ass had hoped for, two hours, just as it was seven months ago. Two hours of pent up passion knotting sheets in perspiration is what I dreamed of just last night, two hours of I love you, I want you, I can't get enough of you. Longer. Faster. Deeper. Harder. The sheet lifts from the feet of our entwine, "I'm sorry," and he rolls on his side away from me as the sheet pulls up to his shoulder. I hear him yawn into the pillow. "I haven't had sex since before I was in jail" I recall him saying in these hungering past few weeks. Seven, maybe eight months now I count. "Never even had a chance to jack, shared a cell with seven guys, a shower with thirteen." I eroticized the thought until he shot the fantasy down an edge. "Ain't like no porn flick in there either. Men never have sex up there in 850 Bryant Special Populations." His tone bitters his memory. Special populations was for inmates with mental health issues or for murderers waiting to be tried. We fall asleep; the naked spoon of men in the afternoon sun, the sheet outlining his curves, my sharp bones. His come drips down the cheek of my ass. Clean sheets and I don't give a fuck.

    My heart jumps me awake. Cold is the space Darnell laid. The time! The time!   What time is it? Gotta get Darnell back to rehab. Where is he? Hey, where is he? Panic shoves my heart into my throat. My scramble from the bed is too quick to call his name, my eyes sweep the room. A dash to the archway into the kitchen is a two step leap. Darnell stands, arms stretched to the window frame, cigarette burning between two fingers, white smoke curling around his naked brown skin. "You alright?" I breathe relief. My question walks me to him.

    "Fine." His words are the distance of his stare, dismissive at being interrupted.   "Gotta get going though." Darnell turns, kisses me softly on the cheek as he passes into the main room, picking up his scattered clothing from the floor. I walk to the window where desire is left lingering in his wake. Crack dealers in black hoodies, addicts' speedy exchanges, a non-stop stream of soiled clothing and green dollar bills, flames sparking cupped hands in the late afternoon blue. I wonder how long he stood here watching them. I wonder why.

"Do you still love me?" Darnell asks on Monday.
"Of course I do man. Why do you ask?"
"Just curious." I read his mind, him reading my past, all of which I have shared with him shamelessly.
"Are you going to date someone after I get my new place?" Darnell asks on Tuesday.
"What do you mean by that?"
"Maybe you want someone more stable, more successful, more endowed."
"Fuck. I am dating you. Other men with other qualities don't interest me." Exasperated I retrieve a beer. I lift it twice and it is empty.
Wednesday night, "Are you seeing one of my ex's?"
"What makes you think that? You know where I am twenty-four seven."
"My ex Monroe has his ways, will try to break us up." Shaking my head I leave the room.
On Thursday night Darnell hits the last chord, "When you masturbate, who do you think about? One of your ex's? Marcene? Stanley? James?"
"Enough!" I slam out of the apartment and push down the hall, irritation is his paranoia lifting the hair of my neck. Guilt is the defensive shame tightening my shoulders as I go, anger is the momentum running my feet down the seven flights of stairs, turning, turning, turning until nearly dizzy in the lobby.
Walking home I forget why I came out. Mad I recall, I am supposed to be mad at Darnell. About what? The afternoon's Fernet seems to have softened the edge. All I want is for his strong arms to hold me. I don't want to be fucked, I don't want to talk about

what angers me, I just want to be held and promised a second chance when I screw up, when I am stupid, when I am wrong. I have only had a couple of men in my life that dared to stick around for more than a couple of years. How long will Darnell put up with me?

ELEVEN

"Five-0!! Five-0!!" It's three a.m., the drug mule shouts the black and white turning the corner; paid in crack, wrapped in self importance, feeling protected, out my fucking window. Three a.m., Darnell's side of the bed lies empty, the pillow at my side a shallow impression where he lay laughing just an hour ago. His drunken words shortly after one a.m. nerve my trembling mind, "Gotta see if my check came." Gone he went to the ATM, his first disability check directly deposited on the first day of the month, cash poor far too long, poverty must have ran him every step of the way.

"Five-0!! Five-0!!" Clenching Darnell's pillow to me I realize I am still drunk, even my thoughts seem to slur. He'll be back in a minute. We celebrated hard last night; the New Year, his first check, housing a promise with a maybe next week hole in it; dinner and clubbing, beer and Jell-O shots simply because they were free and we had never had them before. Celebrated hard all the while desiring rushes beyond the surrounding drunkards, Auld Lang Syne and the rip of heavy metal guitars racing above it.

And all for what? The thought creeps in. Gone in one check I think to myself. Then again he wouldn't do that. Or would he? Something must have happened. I should go looking for him. But where? I drift in worried wonder of him; smoking crack in the shadows, having sex with any hot desire taking notice of him. I worry him pacing his rambling and delusional mind in jail, lying on a gurney in the hospital, beat up, overdosed or waiting to be carted off to the psyche unit. Round and round goes my fucking mind. "Five-0!! Five-0!! Five-0!!"

"FUCK YOU!!" I bolt upright in bed. "FUCK YOU!!" I scream at Darnell,   "FUCK YOU!!" I scream at the mule, I scream at my relentless mind. "Fuck you." I mumble pathetic at whomever; my aim is lost in a rush of dizziness and a heart beating hard to sob. Gone, the fucker is gone. In my drunk beer sadness I plant my feet on the hardwood floor, raising my eyes slowly, inhaling hopes of finding Darnell there tossed among the furniture, discarded clothes and shoes. I exhale into the unforgiving silence. Silver light cuts the room from the shine of the moon. Truth cuts me like shards of glass.   Played. After all I have done, played. Gone. All the, 'I love you's' these past many months fucking sacked, a crack pipe rolling, a dealer counting Darnell's dollars, paranoia trembling, anxiety pushing. My bed is empty. I fucking hate self pity. I am so fucking stupid. He will be back in a minute. I throw the pillow hard into the wall.

I crack a cold one in the kitchen, you would think the refrigerator light would become less blinding through the years. I should have seen this coming. I trouble through my mind the number of times I have found Darnell focused out this kitchen window down to the huddled men and women smoking crack in the shelter from the wind; a doorway, a garage entrance, behind a tree. "Whatcha lookin' at?" I'd ask him full on knowing the answer.

"Oh I thought I knew them." And if you did? I wondered to myself. I bit my sarcasm back, stood behind him on each occasion and wrapped my arms around his slimming waistline hoping distraction would cut the yearning, fearing the place his dishonesty would lead him.

I swig my beer staring out into the cold night. Any minute.

I hear the echo of those streets calling to him, shouting at him, pulling on the sleeve of his hoodie, trying to take his hand; I fight being pulled along with him. Each time we go walking those big ole eyes of his take in the shuffle and the hustle of the Tenderloin a little bit more, dealers step into him in his stride with pointing chins asking without words how much he wants. Easy, they make it seem so damn easy, so matter of fact. We brush on by with eyes straight ahead, it doesn't seem like Darnell breathes. I know I don't. The dealers go chasing another dollar down the street. We brace ourselves for the next offer, the next clutter of men or women heading our way with the cloud of crack hustle dusting their casual stroll.

    Beer drunk, the sadness overtakes me. I read in the paper the other day if beer makes you depressed then consider switching to vodka or gin with something bubbly like soda or tonic to lift your spirits; nothing better than a fucking happy alcoholic. Instead I reach for another. "Five-0!! Five-0!!" It must be four a.m. Any minute now.

TWELVE

January doesn't leave San Francisco. Rain doesn't fall; it seems to just hang in the air. I leave my apartment only when I have to because even with an umbrella the jeans of my legs are soaked, my hands ache the cold, thin soled boots slip on slick metal sidewalk basement doors; willy goes my stomach, the fear of the fall. Each day grays into another. My smile doesn't mean much. Indifference cups my heart. It's the morning. I haven't slept. I stare at Darnell's curl in bed; even covered by blankets I know his lonely, his arms cry for cuddling, the warmth of my body has always been his safety. He promised he would never binge again. He had to. After all he been through, jail, rehab, a new man-responsibility, he couldn't stop. Or so he said. It was then January began to rain. I stare out the window. Never again. I stare at him now, asleep for two days. He gets up to piss, shit, and eat leftovers he doesn't bother to warm.

THIRTEEN

I don't want to die alone; I say half aloud shuddering the thought of it, trying to shake it off, yet the thinking persists. How many days will I lie here before they find me? Just like that friend of mine Kevin, fucker O.D.'d on sleeping pills and it took his roommates a week and a half to realize he wasn't coming out of his room for coffee in the morning. My friend Les always wanted to die well fed and well fucked and he did. After dinner, after he shot his load, after his date said good night and was out the door, Les died alone of a heart attack. He was only forty-six.

Shit, will the stench of my corpse be the alarm to the neighbors I am lying dead in here? Will it be the old hateful, red faced, alcoholic building manager who barred Darnell from coming into the building again? That would be good, ruin his fucking day. Or will the sexy Middle Eastern men at the corner store report me missing when I don't show up for my every day six-pack or on those occasions when I go back for a second sixer and flirt shamelessly with those big brown eyes and olive skin? Alone and dead I shudder, that's how they'll find me, alone and fucking dead.

    Wandering to the bathroom I think back a month, Christmas morning, Darnell and I wake up after sex it seems, a wet dream, a fantasy, a silent erotic film, not a word spoken between us just predawn male carnivorous desires devouring the flesh of each other in black silhouettes against a warming cobalt blue sky. Over these weeks past, Darnell reclaims the sexual prowess which drugs me addicted to him. No man has ever touched me the way he touches me, his hands, his tongue, his eyes, his dick, his attention, his desire to please. I swim in the pleasure he gives me, I drown with no desire to be saved. We lay now, my head on his chest, rising and falling with each inhale, exhale.

    Christmas. A month ago. "Merry Christmas." He side eyes me like he's checking me out. Pulling away from the warmth of his arms and chest I reach to the stack of books on my nightstand, Hubert Selby Jr., James Baldwin, Richard Wright, William Faulkner. "I know we agreed no presents but here." He gives me the shouldn't-have look. I shrug my shoulders. Christmas is his, him being from that long line of preachers. Christmas sure as hell ain't mine. The thought of God left me a long time ago. I hand him two thin books of Anne Sexton's poetry, Darnell's favorite. "Call it happy graduation." Darnell completed his ninety days in rehab just two weeks ago. "Nothing big. Found them in a thrift store." Darnell holds them up to the gathering blue light of day, his smile shines white as his eyes dash out the window to another place, another time; he begins reciting without opening the books held like prayers between his palms,

> *Once more*
> *the sun roaming on the carpenter's back*
> *as he puts joist to sill*
> *and occasionally he looks to the sky*
> *as even the hen when it drinks*
> *looks toward heaven*

Five minutes, ten minutes, fifteen minute pass who knows. The words falling from his lips I don't even hear, can't even listen to as his naked rounded torso breathes each image alive and enduring. To be loved by him as he loves the strength of each word spoken is all I wish for, to be thought of with that same gleam to his eye would turn this ruin of my life into something worth living for. "I love you baby." He falls back into me once the poem or poems ends are reached. "Thank you." He mans himself on the pillows raising the curve of his arm signaling me to cuddle him there with my head on his chest. Now rested, sun lifting, he opens the first pages of the book of 'The Awful Rowing Toward God,' and begins to read. Coffee, apple juice, scrambled eggs, sausage, pancakes with maple syrup, drink, eat, and belch with the turning of the poems until done is done and the lines blur our thoughts. The books closed at his side, he drifts, "She killed herself ya know."

"How?" My enthusiastic intrigue catches his eye on me. Tales of suicide reap my attention. I always want to know how. Why is always the same story.

"Started her car in her garage and let it run. Carbon monoxide poisoning."

"Huh."

"She wore her fur coat." Darnell smirks impressed or amused, checks me for my reaction. My smile remains the entire day.

Christmas, a month ago.

Sitting now the edge of the bed, Darnell has not moved. Yes I am old. The tears come in a slow burning wave, blurring eyes. Never again. My tears fall. I want you forever.

Metal hits the door again; steel knuckle comes rapping. "Goddamn it!" I jump out of bed. Darnell stirs. I stomp to the door smelling grease as I go. "What?! What the fuck?!"

The old man down the hall stands there, droopy sag of an eye pleading me his walker between us, Foley catheter bag swinging the low aluminum bar. He denies my anger lifting a bottle of corn oil up to me, "Son, can ya open this for me?" I open it, hand it back to him. His gnarled hands can't grasp it firm.

"Come on." I step in front of him and walk towards his door with the squeak of his walker trailing after me.

"My nurse didn't show up!"

"The one you fired?" Over my shoulder. I hear he fires them regularly.

"Huh?" I push through his closed-over door as I am hit with a wave of thin smoke and grease burning air.

"Fuck old man, what the fuck are you doing?!" My legs are long and quick into the kitchen where the frying pan sits burning grease on the stove top. I shut off the flame. "Fuck! You trying to burn us all down?"

"It just got a little too hot that's all." His walker squeaks right past me. I slam the oil on the counter and head for the door convinced I will die alone in my burning apartment.

FOURTEEN

    Our two grown men bodies cling a single plastic mattress. Every movement is a slick bottom sheet slide. The fitted corners pop, I tuck them in, they pop again. When I roll away the wall is closer than I expect it to be; the opposite direction Darnell's face is soft, warm. Our faces so close, his exhale hot, my yawn gasps for cool air. He tells me my beer breath is nasty. I still love tobacco on his. My man, his new place, our hope for him to get the chance to stand the man he is. He wants to make his mama proud.
    We bought a blanket at the Goodwill for three, forty-nine; I remembered an old set of sheets the bottom of a trunk back in my studio. Our pillow is the cushion of a short back couch we found on the landing of the stairs down his hall, four inches thick; I managed a pillow case around it. I'd probably sleep

better without the cushion; my neck stretches and finds no comfort. I press the pillow down, I push my shoulder into it to no relief; I am sure I will wake with a kink. Darnell doesn't seem to mind. An hour passes. He snores. His dreams are active conversations he mumbles now and again; I should have brought ear plugs. Romantic I keep telling myself.

The Ambassador Hotel; Darnell's new home, a Direct Access to Housing program. Each week of these past six months we have waited and hoped for a call. I just wanted something good for him, something to faith him through. But a lost application, another form, another background check, a forgotten signature, an interview please stumbled us along until the call came and Darnell's shoulders became wide and strong again, his face filled with hope, his eyes smiled at last. He was lit when he told me he had his own bathroom. I cringed when he said it was the Ambassador.

I did not know how I would be coming back to this hotel. I did not mention to Darnell this was the site where I managed Grayson three years ago. Darnell and I walked past what was once Clarice's office, the office where Grayson shouted his initial hatred of me into the world, the office he was later fired from. These are the halls where he probably first smelled gun powder, set his sight, cocked the trigger and shook with the burning fantasizing rush of having a shotgun in his hands. His hatred spilled from the Ambassador out into the streets, rushing in torrents through the months ahead until he found me in my new office on Ninth Street. I did not breathe in my passing of the closed door, Clarice's office. My stomach hurt I held it so tight. My gaze dropped quick watching the linoleum of the floor beneath my feet go by. In Darnell's sleep he pulls me closer to him. I close my eyes and breathe the memory to pass.

"WHORE! BITCH! CUNT! I AM NONE OF THESE!!" The shrill of a woman's voice outside Darnell's door slaps me awake. "I AM MY OWN LIBERATED WOMAN!!" A door slams, the wall jumps. The door opens again, banging against Darnell's, "DO NOT! I REPEAT, DO NOT, PIMP ME OUT!!" The door slams shut again. I wonder if she is alone. I wonder if she is in danger. I listen close. Her ranting is muffled by the walls, the bathroom and closet between us and her; still her anguish spills over these boundaries. My caution is alert. Darnell stirs but does not wake. A thud, a moan, a heavy sadness in the silence, the window rattling open, the hollow of cupboard doors slam open and shut; I wait for another outburst but minutes pass to maybe an hour. I hear the bass of music. Unease is the silent anxiety in the night. In my mind of a year plus past, I see Darnell on the street corner screaming just like she. I cannot go back there again. I cannot let him go there again. My arms of protection wrapping him is something never known to me.

My eyes stare the ceiling unable to drift away again and I wander along my thoughts; Darnell and I have slept together every day for six months. My heart goes staccato at the thought of sleeping without him; the thought of waking to an empty bed, the trouble of comfort without what I know, his arm, his neck, his chest, the wrap of our legs. Six months of safety is eternity, one night without him a wound exposed to air. Before Darnell so many nights were dark empty caves of uncertainty. So many nights I would enter them fearing I would not wake at dawn. I bury no into his neck. I beg please into my bite of his flesh. I need my man. I need to wake up in the morning in our well of clammy masculinity; the salty ripe earth of pits and crotches, the mulch of men, the groans of conquering dreams ending. I need the heat of him, the strength of his arms. To sleep without him is love without fucking thunder.

Sirens scream the night. I sleep but wake again and again. I worry about Darnell here at the Ambassador, alone with that crazy woman as his neighbor. How many nights a week does she go shouting like she does? I see his eyes wide in their fear of her and I wonder if he is too close to the fire. I travel in my mind down the hall wondering who else lives here, wondering who will come knocking on his door. Are they all as crazy as she? I exhaust the thought. I am so fucking stupid. I am in the Tenderloin, in a fucking subsidized SRO. Who the fuck do I think lives here? They won't come knocking for a cup of sugar.

Three steps from the Ambassador the corner of Turk and Taylor threatens. In the dense of milling bodies the front of a five dollar crack rock today is a payback of ten tomorrow. One day later it is fifteen. The lure of escape begs Darnell; I know this just watching his eyes, tasting his appetite. It could be a high-end cup cake up on Union Square, a rush of Pop Tarts and Twinkies instead. It could be multiple orgasms, multiple men, a Sunday bucket of Kentucky Fried Chicken, a pint of cheap scotch. All of these take him somewhere other than here. My fear of him going leaves me abandoned simply in the thought. The voice of my therapist from two weeks past is the cold of one still moment. "You must learn to love detached, know he will use again, accept that, draw a circle around yourself and take care of only what lies within that circle." The problem is, when I hold Darnell as close as I do now he is inside my circle, I in his.

My ears go listening but all is silent next door, silent down the hall. I turn my attention to the valley of the inner block Darnell's window opens out to. A sea of red brick buildings shake and hum through the night, open windows, different music from different systems, different TV's on different stations, a symphony of chaos, an occasional shout undefined. I am swept with the feeling of sorrow and struggle, humbled imagining how many times hope has lifted a man from his single bed in his single room to his step and stride of survival.

Made in the USA
San Bernardino, CA
12 August 2014